Conway Public Library

4551 00128834

W9-AZS-874

8.18

Date Due

SEP 1 7 2018		
OCT 1 0 2018		
NOV 0 6 2018		
NOV 2 0 2018		
DEC 1 0 2018		
JAN 3 1 2019		

BRODART, CO.   Cat. No. 23-233   Printed in U.S.A.

Praise for Hearts of the Fathers

A Masterpiece! A "must read" for every American. With prophetic insight, Chuck uncovers the overlooked issue of "fatherlessness" and its grave, devastating effect upon our country. There is no more urgent book that needs to be read, heeded and taken to heart than *Hearts of the Fathers* by Chuck Crismier.

—WILLIAM J. FEDERER, BESTSELLING AUTHOR

Great book. In this present day, our need for godly fathers is greater than ever. Chuck challenges us and reminds us that we cannot delay our calling. Now is the time. Time waits for no man to ensure leaving a legacy that can last. Time proves men. Truly, we need a generation of champions, strong and valiant, who will rise up for the times . . . if we are to leave a lasting legacy.

—DOUG STRINGER, FOUNDER/PRESIDENT, SOMEBODY CARES
AMERICA, SOMEBODY CARES INTERNATIONAL

In his newest book, Chuck Crismier rightfully proclaims "If the hearts of the children are to be turned back toward their fathers, the minds of the fathers must first be renewed." This book is a virtual treasure-trove of comparable transforming truths, demanding that you read it with a highlighter in hand. *Hearts of the Fathers* sizzles with conviction, instruction, prophetic insight and hope. We. Needed. This. Book!

—CARL GALLUPS, SENIOR PASTOR, BEST-SELLING AUTHOR

At a time when fatherlessness has become a national epidemic, in both the culture and in the church, there could not be a more timely book that *Hearts of the Fathers*. This book will help to transform your family! I highly recommend every pastor who desires to raise up men as spiritual leaders read this book and apply its truths and practices."

—DR. ROBERT JEFFRESS, SENIOR PASTOR FIRST BAPTIST CHURCH
DALLAS, TEXAS

Charles Crismier has done an amazing job reminding us of the importance of earthly, mortal fathers, the role of God as our Father, the amazing prophecy of Malachi about turning the hearts of fathers back to their children and the hearts of children back to their fathers, as well as the world's absolute war on fathers. Poignant, timely, relevant and engaging. The right message at the right time.

—JOSEPH FARAH, FOUNDER AND CEO, WND

A book all men should read, whether a father or not, as our country is in need of returning to a legacy of virtue, character, loving discipline and pursuit of Truth. Very powerful and convicting. Chuck Crismier lays out a return path for a legacy renewed in our children.

—TOM COBURN MD, UNITED STATES SENATOR-OK, RETIRED

Hearts of the Fathers is a powerful, passionate, practical and Biblical call to action. If you're a parent, a grandparent, or someone who works with children, you need to read this book!

—DR. DAVID CLARKE, CHRISTIAN PSYCHOLOGIST, SPEAKER, AUTHOR

Hearts of the Fathers is a much-needed book for families today. Crismier calls fathers to fully engage in their God-given role. This book will also help mothers and children understand God's original plan for the family with a greater appreciation for the responsibility and roles of fathers. These truths will inspire dads to put down the remote and get off the couch to rise up in intentionally passing on a legacy of faith to the next generation.

—MELISSA SPOELSTRA, CONFERENCE SPEAKER AND AUTHOR OF
TOTAL FAMILY MAKEOVER: 8 STEPS TO MAKING DISCIPLES AT HOME

This book will not only be an excellent resource for men who want to fully understand and faithfully execute their role as fathers but it will also serve as a robust tool to help pastors and men's leaders guide their men to live and lead as the faithful fathers (both biological and spiritual) that many younger men desperately seek.

—MIKE YOUNG, FOUNDER, NOBLE WARRIORS

Superb book. Chuck Crismier speaks mostly to husbands and fathers but also to the Church, and the nation, not as a counselor, lawyer, or pastor (all of which he is) but as a prophet. He cuts into our very hearts as men—dividing between the soul and spirit, laying bare our hearts and exposing our failures and inadequacies with the raw truth of God's word. He demonstrates that most modern men don't understand even the basics of fatherhood. No psychological approach here. "Hearts" challenges men to repent and arise: first, to know "Our Father," ("from Whom every family on heaven and earth is named" – Eph 3:15), then to become the fathers He intends us to be, then to do our part to restore Biblical fatherhood to our churches and nation. Our abandon of Biblical fatherhood is at the root of many, if not most of our societal ills. May God use *Hearts of the Fathers*, fast moving, yet Biblically comprehensive and filled with important facts and figures, to awaken men (and women) everywhere to become God pleasers who will raise godly sons and daughters, who will exemplify God's way in their own marriages and families, and who will be used by God to help save and restore the foundational institutions of fatherhood, marriage and family to our culture. These institutions were born out of the heart, person and character of God, Himself, and are utterly essential to the survival of our nation, indeed, to the survival of civilization itself. May God bless those who read this book.

—REV. PIERRE BYNUM, CHAPLAIN & NATIONAL PRAYER DIRECTOR
FAMILY RESEARCH COUNCIL

CHARLES CRISMIER

hearts
of the
fathers

LEAVING A LEGACY THAT LASTS

 WND Books

248.8
Crism, C.

hearts *of the* fathers

Copyright © 2018 by Charles Crismier

All rights reserved. No part of this book may be reproduced in any form or by any means—whether electronic, digital, mechanical, or otherwise—without permission in writing from the publisher, except by a reviewer, who may quote brief passages in a review.

Published by WND Books, Washington, D.C. WND Books is a registered trademark of WorldNetDaily.com, Inc. ("WND"). Published in conjunction and cooperation with Elijah Books, the author's independent publishing arm.

Book designed by Mark Karis

WND Books are available at special discounts for bulk purchases. WND Books also publishes books in electronic formats. For more information call (541) 474-1776, e-mail orders@wndbooks.com or visit www.wndbooks.com.

Hardcover ISBN: 978-1-944229-92-4
eBook ISBN: 978-1-944229-93-1

Library of Congress Cataloging-in-Publication Data Available Upon Request

Printed in the United States of America
17 18 19 20 21 22 MPV 9 8 7 6 5 4 3 2 1

With fatherly fondness and a deep sense of gratitude to the Father, I dedicate these words to my children and grandchildren; to my dear wife, who has consistently encouraged and facilitated our relationships; and to all fathers whose lives have been or will be influenced toward leaving a godly and lasting legacy.

—CHUCK CRISMIER,
FATHER, GRANDFATHER, AND DISCIPLER OF MEN

Contents

the father's heart for fathers

GIVE EAR, O my people . . . to the words of my mouth . . . which we have . . . known, and our fathers have told us.

WE WILL NOT HIDE THEM from [our] children, sh[o]wing to the generation to come the praises of the LORD, and his strength, and his wonderful works that he hath done.

FOR HE ESTABLISHED A TESTIMONY . . . and appointed a law . . . which he commanded our fathers, that they should make them known to their children:

THAT THE GENERATION TO COME might know them, even the children which should be born; who should arise and declare them to their children;

THAT THEY MIGHT SET THEIR HOPE in God, and not forget the works of God, but keep his commandments:

AND MIGHT NOT BE AS THEIR FATHERS, a stubborn and rebellious generation . . . whose spirit was not steadfast with God [the Father].

—PSALM 78:1-8

now is our time: a passionate plea to fathers

FIRST AS A LAWYER AND BUSINESSMAN, I have been speaking passionately to men for nearly forty years from coast to coast. Near the end of the twentieth century, I became strongly impressed to warn God's people of the difficult and challenging times coming upon the earth. Of particular concern were my American countrymen who profess the name of Christ in a nation proudly religious yet profoundly undiscipled.

As founder of Save America Ministries in 1992 and as host of *VIEWPOINT*, a daily, issues-oriented radio broadcast since 1995, a deep sense of concern about the spiritual condition of my brothers in Christ increasingly threatened to overwhelm me. The weight of the burden began to take its toll in my own physical health. Over a period of three to four years, as health deteriorated with the mounting stress from the developing picture of a spiritually backslidden nation, I came face to face with the reality that, despite daily reasoning, wooing and warning by radio, I could not change the heart of those who claim the name of Christ. Only God, by His Spirit, can change a man's heart. I was a mere messenger.

During the last twenty-three years, I have been privileged to interview over three thousand Christian and national leaders, authors and broadcasters on *VIEWPOINT*. Since I often frame daily issues confronting our hearts and homes in the context of rapidly developing end-time events, I have explored with a number of guests their own viewpoint on the preparedness of professing Christians in America for Christ's Second Coming.

I have inquired of pastoral and para-church leaders what percentage of those professing to be Christians in our country they believe to be prepared for our Lord's return. Shockingly, the average response has been only 10 percent. The responses have ranged from 5 percent to 15 percent. How does this strike you? To me it is frightening! And what does it say of our children . . . of the rest of the nation . . . and of our spiritual impact upon the "unbelieving" world?

According to a recent Gallup Poll, 45 percent of Americans claim to be either born-again or evangelical Christians, yet our spiritual leaders find only 5 to 15 percent of these are living lives ready to face Christ at His return. The potential consequences are staggering. Terrifying!! And what does it say of fathers?

We are being set up for massive deception, giving all new meaning to Jesus' words, "Strait is the gate, and narrow is the way, which leadeth to life, and *few there be that find it*" (Matt. 7:14). Yet the prevailing message by many pastors and para-church leaders across the land is an ear-tickling message of the moment, pandering to self-interest while bowing to the shrine of the Market. We are not, by and large, discipling God's people and our own children for eternal destiny, but instead are engaged in a temporal do-si-do with the culture. Frighteningly, the fear of the Lord has been virtually abandoned as our foundation of biblical faith crumbles. And we men are painfully complicit.

It is in this context I write with a passion born of urgency. Time is running out. For several years I have labored with the growing conviction that God's people, especially men, desperately need to be warned of the massive and multiplied deceptions now rapidly sweeping the earth. The time is now! But what must we do?

To write about deception is a daunting task, for the breadth of the problem is vast and the scope of potential deceptions is enormous. To attempt to identify and articulate all is impossible. The best that can be done is to present an orderly and principled framework for identifying various forms of deception and their delivery systems and to prepare the mind and heart of men to identify falsehood and embrace truth. This formidable task I sought to accomplish in the release of *SEDUCTION of the Saints* in 2009, and, in *The SECRET of the Lord*, (2011). Now, in *Hearts of the Fathers* I am seeking to restore to spiritual memory a singular truth that will open a door of genuine hope in the midst of the imploding global horror that is rapidly enslaving the earth, disguised in the garb of a false faith promising peace and prosperity.

It is said that fools rush in where angels fear to tread. That is particularly true when areas of potential deception cross over into or invade realms of doctrine and personal life practices. I acknowledge that I approach those discussions with considerable trepidation. Yet the life practices we embrace oftentimes have unintended or unconsidered consequences that may lead people into deception or into a false sense of security, deterring them from shoring up already weakened walls of spiritual defense. I ask for God's grace and your mercy as we continuously pick our way through some of these life minefields.

Read the pages that follow prayerfully. Be open to the Holy Spirit's tug on your own heart and mind. Remember men, we are dealing with matters of destiny . . . eternal destiny. Let us prepare the way of the Lord together, restoring the *HEARTS of the Fathers*, beginning in each of our own hearts, just as THE FATHER now pleads with a broken Fatherly heart. This is our time!

Yours for a Revived Church,
a Restored Nation,
and Prepared Fathers,

—CHARLES CRISMIER

1

TITANIC PROPHECY

A tale of haunting deception hovering over history's most remembered disaster.

THE LIGHTS FLICKERED OUT, and in a thunderous roar, everything on the super-ship seemed to break loose. Beds and boilers lurched as the black hull of the RMS *Titanic* tilted perpendicularly; its three great propellers reared against the heavens. And then it was gone, and 1522 souls with it.

Fathers and grandfathers, Christian and pagan, went down to the depths of history together. But what legacy did they leave? Business-as-usual lifetime decisions and destiny converged in a single, gut-wrenching moment where truth took on "titanic" proportions. What tale will be told when history and prophecy converge in the eternal tally of failed fatherhood as we rapidly approach the biblical moment of truth in our own valley of decision? What will be the heavenly Father's view of our legacy?

There had been no sense of urgency when the *Titanic* first

struck an iceberg in the North Atlantic at about 11:40 PM on April 14, 1912. When Edith Brown Haisman last saw her daddy, he was standing on deck, smoking a cigar and smiling at his wife and daughter. "I'll see you in New York," he said confidently, as his family was bundled into Lifeboat No. 14. "Everyone kept saying, 'She's unsinkable'," recalled Haisman.[1] But the *unthinkable* happened to the "unsinkable." Emerging from the depths of the sea and lifeboat survivors is a tale of haunting deception and undisclosed secrets hovering over history's most remembered disaster.

"A NIGHT TO REMEMBER"

It was "A Night to Remember" said Walter Lord in his classic 1955 best seller. But the *Titanic* was by no means the largest disaster in modern history. Unlike the *Lusitania* and the *Hindenburg*, it had virtually no political import. "Yet it remains the only disaster that people generally care about." Stephen Cox, author of *The Titanic Story*, asks, "What is there about the Titanic story that keeps us coming back to it? What is the significance of this story?" "You can have a real story without risks, but the best stories are those that ask the riskiest questions about good and bad. When we try to answer them, we recover our sense of dignity of human life. . . . That's why we keep coming back to the *Titanic* story—because it makes us think about the things that matter."[2]

It is little wonder, then, that historian Steven Biel in his reminiscing cultural history of the disaster, *Down with the Old Canoe*, speculates that "The three most written-about subjects of all-time" may be "Jesus, the Civil War, and the *Titanic*."[3]

"Buried 12,000 feet beneath the sea in total darkness, gone

from a world it momentarily defined, the *Titanic* refuses to die."
"It's a morality play," observed *Newsweek,* "a biblical warning to
those who would dare to challenge the Almighty."[4]

"WE'RE ALL ON THE TITANIC"

It remains a night to forget for those who were on board, but
a night to remember for the world. It is an irresistible tale of
tragedy and truth. "Seventeen movies, eighteen documentaries
and at least 130 books have attempted to reveal the moral and
spiritual mysteries played out in the drama of deception played
out before the world on the decks of the *Titanic.* "

"It's a moment in time that encapsulates what life is all
about," said Tullock, of RMS Titanic, Inc.[5] The *Titanic* wasn't
annihilated in an instant. It took two hours and forty minutes to
sink, during which people—rich and poor, young and old—had
to make choices.

They also, in a condensed moment of lifetime reflection,
experienced either great peace or profound lament for the
legacy they would leave. "It is an interesting fact that newspaper
reports, magazine articles and books published shortly after the
Titanic's sinking referred to eternal truths," wrote Bob Garner,
senior producer for Focus on the Family. Yet "most of these
were secular publications," he noted. Garner had been a working
associate of Dr. Robert Ballard, who first discovered the remains
of the great ship in 1985, resting two miles down on the ocean
floor in the cold, pitch blackness of the North Atlantic.[6]

There are pivotal points in our lives when we are brought
face-to-face with the things in life that matter most. At those
junctures are choices that must be made, choices that inevitably
determine the course of destiny. Deception and undisclosed

secrets deliver us to the brink of destiny. "It's a metaphor" for life, observed James Cameron, director of the extravaganza film production in 1996. In a very real sense, "We're all on the "*Titanic.*"[7]

THE "UNSINKABLE"

The *Titanic* was large even by today's standards. This was the grandest of the grand, "representing all the power, wealth, luxury and arrogance of its age." "The *Titanic* was built at the height of the Industrial Age, a time when technology ruled as a 'god'." She was promoted as "unsinkable," with her sixteen watertight compartments. Several passengers wrote in their diaries that they overheard people claim, "even God couldn't sink this ship."[8]

Yet the *unthinkable* happened to the "unsinkable." One deception led to another. Undisclosed secrets obscured what might otherwise have seemed obvious. Passengers boarded, brashly confident in the safety of their families. The ill-fated Capt. Edward J. Smith was also boldly confident, cranking up the speed to set a new trans-Atlantic speed record, even as the regal vessel approached the well-known North Atlantic ice fields. Unbeknownst to unsuspecting passengers, no safety drills had been conducted. Fathers were oblivious to the most basic safety precautions for their families.

The wireless operators ignored or made light of repeated warnings of icebergs ahead. Even the captain seemed complacent. At about 11PM, when the ship's crew spotted "iceberg ahead," frantic orders were given to turn the massive liner. There are few more dramatic or spine-tingling lines in the history of cinema than those of the *Titanic* captain in an earlier film when, upon news of "iceberg dead ahead," he cries pleadingly to his ship, "turn," "Turn," "TURN!" exclaiming, "Dearest God!" And upon news of having struck the berg, he utters softly, "Impossible!"

Yet the deception continued. Even though a three-hundred foot slice a little over a quarter inch wide was scraped by the ice through the hull, nothing was detectible by anyone on board. But the "unsinkable" ship had been mortally wounded. Yet even that fact remained a virtual secret, and fathers made little effort to secure those that trusted them by seeking the truth of what was happening.

FATHERS LEFT BEHIND

Still, nothing was detected by the passengers on board, even as the "watertight" compartments filled with water. Few had any clue what was happening. Many joked even when ordered to begin boarding lifeboats. Not until the "unsinkable" began listing and tilting did passengers realize they were in trouble. That which long seems "secret" inevitably surfaces to the surprise of the unsuspecting, leaving little time to take stock of reality.

"It was dreadful," remembered Eva Hart, a seven-year-old survivor who, with her mother, was put on a lifeboat as her father was left behind. She could hear the screams echoing across the freezing waters as the huge ship rose, and suddenly slipped below, and all was darkness. "It was absolutely dreadful," she lamented.[9]

And so it will be when the consequences of creeping spiritual deception become manifested in our lives as we approach the end of the age. Pomp, pride, power, perks, and position keep our spirits falsely afloat while this great "unsinkable" ship of earth takes on water, ready to plunge into the abyss where time and eternity meet. The overwhelming majority will be deceived. Secrets that seduced will surface too late. Their destiny will be determined. Their mournful cries will be deafening. The *unthinkable* will happen to the *unsinkable*. It will be dreadful. Absolutely dreadful. Yet there is a key—a missing key—especially for fathers.

THE MISSING KEY

"It looked for all the world like an ordinary key, but this unremarkable piece of metal could have saved the *Titanic* from disaster." Such were the opening words in a heart-rending report of remorse in the *Telegraph* online paper published in the United Kingdom August 30, 2007.[10]

Catastrophically for the *Titanic* and her 1522 passengers that lost their lives, the key's owner, the Second Officer, David Blair, was removed from the crew at the last minute, and in his haste, forgot to hand it to his replacement. The key is thought to have fitted the locker that contained the crow's nest binoculars, vital to detecting lurking threats to the liner in pre-sonar days. Without the glasses, lookouts in the crow's nest had to rely on their own eyes, which were unable to perceive the disaster lying ahead until it was too late.

A survivor, Fred Fleet, was called by Congress to testify. When asked by the chairing U.S. Senator how much sooner the binoculars would have made the looming iceberg visible, he answered, "Enough to get out of the way."

Ninety-five years later, the key and its significance had truly come to light and was put up for auction. Alan Aldridge, auctioneer, said, "We think this key is one of the most important artifacts from the *Titanic* to come to light." "It is the key that had the potential to save the *Titanic*."

THE SIGNIFICANCE OF PERCEIVED INSIGNIFICANCE

For want of a key, the *Titanic* sank. For lack of a seemingly insignificant piece of metal, the world's greatest luxury liner and most of those who trusted in her safety met their demise. Dreadful! The *unthinkable* happened to the *unsinkable*.

And so it will be as the great ship of this world plunges at breakneck speed, setting new global and economic records, into the freezing and darkening waters of end-time deception. For most, it is not what we know but what we don't know, what remains "secret," that will define a destiny of destruction, both temporally and eternally. Yet we plunge proudly ahead, thinking we are "unsinkable." This is true for both professing believers and unbelievers. Both went down with the *Titanic* for lack of a key.

The key was not truly seen as a significant until after the disaster. Yet it was this seemingly insignificant key that would have provided the clarity of vision and depth of understanding to avoid the deceptively dangerous iceberg that lay ahead.

At this remarkable and unprecedented moment in human history, the greatest and most significant key to avoid personal and collective shipwreck is ignored or deemed relatively insignificant, especially by fathers. The Bible, the very inspired Word of God himself, has become either disregarded or disdained. Yet it alone, insignificant as it may seem in light of mans' titanic achievements, provides the key to life, revealing the dangers lurking not only in the swirling waters around us but in the dark and turbulent waters ahead.

TITANIC'S LAST SECRETS

The world now remembers... again. It has been a century since the *Titanic* met its moment of truth. The tale of terror never ceases to grip our moral and spiritual imagination. Those memories are embellished with a thousand "What if's." Yet another account has now surfaced, probing deeply below the surface discussions and the usually-repeated observations that haunt us to this day. Might there have been a more fundamental "secret" laying undisclosed at the door of *Titanic*'s demise? Enter *Titanic's Last Secret* published in 2008.

This "riveting book weaves new evidence from the depths with historical accounts to reveal dark, hidden truths about the deadly voyage." The "shocking conclusion: What happened aboard the *Titanic* that night was far worse than anyone ever guessed."[11]

In "a fresh, moving, and irresistible portrait of the doomed ship, combining . . . secret archives and forensic engineering . . . Brad Marsden . . . offers haunting new conclusions about *Titanic*: It did not have to happen this way. They did not have to die."[12] But why?

"The true story of *Titanic* has never been told," wrote Tom McCluskie. "I know things nobody else knows."[13] Indeed he did. He had worked at the great shipyard, Harland and Wolf (where *Titanic* was built), from 1965 to 1997. He ended his career as the company archivist, and was the author of four books on Olympic-class ships. His access to shipyard records made him the world's most direct living link to the people who had built *Titanic*.

The *Titanic* had been flawed from its "foundation." The same flaw in its sister ships had become well apparent and major effort was made to retrofit them in order to structurally remedy their deadly affects. Corners had been cut in construction so as to reduce costs of construction as well as continuing costs of coal needed to fuel the required structural weight. Pursuit of profit compromised architectural and engineering principle. And the rest is a wake of horror defining a century of history.

The expansion joints on the deck and hull of the massive *Titanic* were far from adequate. The steel plating called for by the architectural plans was so reduced as to compromise engineering integrity of the vessel. And "every flaw in *Titanic's* hull had stolen minutes from the lives of 1504 people who might otherwise have been rescued by the *Carpathia*."[14]

McCluskie noted: "You don't design two sister ships, you design one. Then you use the same set of plans to build both of them. On the *Titanic* drawings, you can see lots of changes made by Thomas Andrews (the architect) after he discovered design flaws during *Olympic's* sea trials." "*Olympic* must have been right on the edge of coming apart."[15] "Yet *Titanic* was given only one day of sea trial after such troubling discoveries."

What about the British Board of Trade inquiry? "At the inquiry," said McCluskie, "it was a whitewash to reassure the world that British ships were safe."[16] "However, from private documentation within the company which I saw many times, they determined that it was very likely that the ship had broken in half (on the surface). It was never made public."[17]

Pirrie and Ismay, the owner and principal of the *Titanic* project, whose decisions had determined the destiny of so many, "must have been terrified when they'd figured that out [that the known weak joints had caused the "unsinkable" to collapse]. A public discussion of the weaknesses in their Ship of Dreams would have ruined them. They'd had no choice but to keep them secret."[18] Regrettably, pastors and politicians face the very same destiny-determining choices today, and lamentably are following the same course of denial.

COLLISION COURSE WITH DESTINY

We are on a collision course with destiny. Destruction for most lies ahead. Our vision is clouded. Our perspective is limited to our personal or collective earth-bound thoughts, yet the Creator, the Lord of history, knows what lies ahead. He sees what is "secret" to us. The Bible is our binocular. It is the "key" that opens our vision, our hearts and our understanding to see beyond our naked human visual limitations. Yet we, especially fathers, must value the key enough to get out the "binocular" that will enable us to see the dastardly deceptions ahead that lurk below life's surface like a deadly iceberg, waiting to destroy the unwary.

Pastor and people, presidents, potentates and the poor are all on board mans' prideful ship, churning headlong into the darkness of deception. Never in human history have the forces of deception combined with the Devil's demonic host into such a formidable agent of destruction to lead you into perdition. The greatest warnings to you and me come from our Lord himself and from His disciples. The telegraphed warnings are principally to the church, to those who profess to be followers of Christ, and to fathers.

Most will not heed the warnings. The apostle Paul warned that they will be gripped by "strong delusion" and that they will "believe a lie" (II Thess. 2:9-12). Some pastors, through proud and neglectful delay, will, like the Captain of the *Titanic* in a last desperate moment, cry, "Turn," "TURN," *"TURN!"* But it will be too late. They will wince silently in eternal remorse, "Dearest God." "Impossible!"

Most will simply plunge blindly ahead, deceptively convinced of the unsinkability of their ship in which they have idolatrously placed their trust. Hordes will trust the counterfeit Christ for a last great fling on the titanic of earth, spurning the hope and direction promised by Christ, the "Captain of their salvation" (Heb. 2:10), and His seemingly insignificant key. The carnage will be dreadful. Absolutely dreadful!

Don't let it happen to you! The "titanic" prophecy contained in *HEARTS of the Fathers* unlocks the "key" of hope for every father and grandfather who will take it.

YOUR KEY TO AVOID DECEPTION

The Scriptures, known as the Bible or God's Word, provide the "key" to avoid end-time deception. Yet for most its truths remain a virtual "secret." Our problem is not that we fathers do not have the key but that we do not truly and seriously seek its significance so as to properly put it to use in order that we can be guided in our lives to avoid the icebergs of life and the massive deception that now threatens to destroy us.

This book is an effort to take out the "binocular" of God's Word so as to give a more distant and distinct view of the deception now surrounding us and of the profound danger that lies ahead if we, as fathers, do not make timely course correction. Destiny will be determined by the value we place upon God's "key," so as to restore the hearts of the fathers to the children and the children to their fathers.

Remember, the *Titanic* is a metaphor for life. In a significant sense, "We're all on the *Titanic*" together. We may just want to replace the earthly captains in whom we trust with Yeshua, the Messiah, the Christ, who alone is the true "Captain" of our salvation and who alone can guide us as fathers in this particularly desperate moment of history through the multiplied icebergs of deception that threaten shipwreck to our lives, and families. In these choppy waters, *HEARTS of the Fathers* provides the elusive key so that a father need never utter the desperate words... "ICEBERG AHEAD," to his family without hope or prayer.

The "titanic" biblical prophecy of our times, these end times, is ready to be revealed, requiring the response on deck, of every man, father and grandfather before the seeming *unsinkable* becomes the *unthinkable*. The key must first open the door of your heart.

PROBING OUR HEARTS

1. In what way or ways are we "all on the "Titanic?"

2. How is it that the *Titanic* has become a "metaphor for life" for over 100 years?

3. Why are we, as fathers, so easily deceived, often blinding ourselves to the most important things in life?

4. What insights, if revealed timely to listening ears, might have determined a different legacy for 1500 souls?

5. Are you willing to receive and embrace the fatherly "key" that might save those in your sphere of influence?

2

THE DAYS OF ELIJAH

He shall turn the heart of the fathers to the children, and the heart of the children to the fathers.

—MALACHI 4:6

THE "ELIJAH" MESSAGE

No message is more profound or passionately proclaimed from the mouth of the prophet than the "Elijah Message," for it spans the panoply of both Testaments, New and Old. The pure and holy fellowship with God as Father binds the pages of biblical history into a tapestry of love that, when breached, inevitably descends into tragedy. From Adam's treasonous breach in the garden of Eden to Abraham's triumphant obedience on Mount Moriah, from King David's humble trust and relationship as a "man after [God's] own heart" to Christ as obedient Son, who "became the author of eternal salvation unto all them that obey him" (Acts 13:22; Heb. 5:8–9), the Father remains the centerpiece of "the faith once delivered to the saints" (Jude 3).

THE WAR OF TWO WORLDS

It is precisely because this Fatherhood lies at the very root of righteous relationship with Creator God that the enemy of our souls so desperately seeks to destroy the purity of such relationship—indeed, fatherhood itself—thus shifting all allegiance of those made in the image of Father God to the unrepentant rebel "son"—the deceiver—your adversary the devil. This historic war for fatherly allegiance, trust, and obedience is now, in our time, coming to violent culmination. And earthly fathers—indeed, entire families by the millions—have been and are becoming the horrific casualties of this spiritual war, even among those who profess the Father's name. The cumulating carnage is nothing short of catastrophic.

A PASSIONATE WARNING

God, in extreme brokenness of heart, has issued a prophetic and passionate proclamation of wooing and warning worldwide. Four hundred years before the advent of Yeshua Messiah, the Anointed Son, the prophet Malachi pierced the prophetic silence with the "Elijah Message" to our generation. Consider it carefully and prayerfully.

> Behold, I will send you Elijah the prophet before the coming of the great and dreadful day of the LORD.
>
> And he shall turn the heart of the fathers to the children, and the heart of the children to their fathers, lest I come and smite the earth with a curse (Mal. 4:5–6).

THE ETERNAL CONNECTION

It is truly fascinating that the Elijah Message to fathers follows God's lament over the disregard and even rebellion of pastor/priest and people who claim His name as God but who refuse to honor Him as *Father*. From the divine Father's viewpoint, genuine fatherhood on earth disintegrates to the degree that we disregard our relationship with Him as *Father*.

DISASTER IS DESCENDING

The progressive collapse of society ensues, as described in the "Societal Postscript" at the end of this book. Families are breaking apart, children becoming virtual orphans. Mothers and wives have become virtual widows. Poverty of spirit has devolved into economic poverty. Paternal direction wanes and disillusionment prevails. Lawful love has devolved into licentiousness. Feelings have become lord, and faith is faltering.

Absent the consistent love and obedience of faithful fathers, fear is taking hold of the children. The God-ordered earthly anchor for soul security has apostasized. Time approaches eternity as chaos reigns supreme. Society continues to implode in progressive calamity until the curse has fully come.

THE VALLEY OF DECISION

Such is our time. And God, in Fatherly mercy, sends forth "Elijah" the prophet. The "great and dreadful day of the LORD" is upon us (Mal. 4:5–6). And we have serious choices to make, for now and for eternity. "Multitudes, multitudes in the valley of decision: for the day of the LORD is near in the valley of decision" (Joel 3:14). How will we respond? Do we have ears to hear? Do we have the spiritual will to respond to the cry of the Father? Destiny rides in the balance—both temporal and eternal.

PREPARING THE WAY

The Father is determined. Through His mercy and by His Fatherly grace, He yearns for His Creation—but especially those who claim His name—to return before the great day of judgment, "the great and terrible day of the LORD" (Joel 2:21), when true fatherly allegiance and honor are measured and the eternal household is determined. Once, in time past, Elijah the prophet dramatically confronted Israel crying: "How long will you halt between two opinions?" (1 Kings 18:21 AMPC). Again, before the first coming of the Savior, God raised up John the Baptist as "a voice . . . crying in the wilderness" to God's people, "prepare ye the way of the LORD" (Isa. 40:3, John 1:23; Luke 1:17), to "turn the hearts of the fathers." And in ultimate and passionate expression of His fatherly heart, the Father now sends forth the spirit of Elijah with the same and final message to "prepare the way of the Lord" by restoring the hearts of the fathers to the Father and to their children. Indeed, these are *the days of Elijah*. Will we respond any more faithfully or fervently than did ancient Israel? Time and eternity will record our decision. Will we, at last, bring joy to the Father's grieving heart?

Indeed, these are *the days of Elijah*.

THE BIBLE'S FOCUS ON FATHERS

Fathers who want to impress a point on their children see fit to repeat themselves as seems necessary. How frequently has the Father seen fit to emphasize the importance of fatherhood in His Word? The answer is astounding!

"Father"	979 times	in	852 verses
"Fathers"	549 times	in	514 verses
"Forefathers"	2 times	in	2 verses
TOTAL:	1,573 times	in	1,411 verses

PROBING OUR HEARTS

1. In what ways is the Father the centerpiece of the faith once delivered to the saints?

2. Why might fatherhood be under such intense attack in our generation?

3. What are the echoing consequences of fatherlessness and the persistent attacks on fathering in our generation . . . even in the church?

4. What is the Elijah message, and what are its implications?

5. Why might the quality of our relationship with our sons and daughters be connected to our own relationship with the Father?

3

A BROKENHEARTED FATHER

Father!—to God himself we cannot give a holier name.

—WILLIAM WORDSWORTH

GOD IS BROKENHEARTED. He declares Himself to be a *Father*, but His creatures, made in His image, are wayward, indeed rebellious. Even those who claim to be His children—His sons and daughters—have wandered far from the ways of His household. Lamentably, Father's Word is no longer "law" in the household of faith. And God grieves.

WHY GOD GRIEVES

Today – and every day - the God of Creation grieves. But why? He grieves because those who profess to bear His name have refused to walk in His ways. They have, as did Israel of old, rejected His Word, His Will, and His Ways while claiming—insisting upon—the blessings of His household. They "hold the truth in unrighteousness" (Rom. 1:18) while purporting to be His rightful heirs according to His covenant (Ps. 50:16–23). And they . . . no . . . *we* . . . have gone astray.

According to Romans 11, both Jew and Gentile believers have been "concluded in unbelief" and unrighteousness (v. 32). Gentiles, who were given the privilege of being "grafted in" to God's family through the covenant of Abraham, have now, in large measure, turned from the obedience of faith, as did Israel before them (Rom. 16:26). Having been ordained by the Father to "provoke them [Israel] to jealousy" (Rom. 11:11) we have become like stiff-necked Israel in our cavalier disregard of Father's authority in His household, and His Father heart is broken. Broken! Absolutely broken!!!

GRIEF FOR OUR GENERATION

Overwhelming grief envelops the heart of the Heavenly Father. Over and over God lamented over Israel's repeated apostasy. He spoke of their "hardness of heart." He warned of their rebellion that provoked and tempted Him to judge or destroy them. "They do alway[s] err in their heart," cried the Father, "and they have not known my ways," so "they shall not enter into my rest" (Heb. 3:7–11; see Num. 14:28–29). "I was grieved with that generation," He said (Heb. 3:10).

That was *their* generation, but what would the Father of Abraham, Isaac, and Jacob and of our Lord and Savior Jesus Christ (Yeshua the Messiah) say to *our* generation? And of what generation are we?

As Gentile "believers," we claim to be a "chosen generation" (1 Peter 2:9), but so did they. They claimed to be heirs according to Father's covenant, as do we (Rom. 8:17). If Father was grieved so deeply with that generation, the original "olive tree," would not His grief—and warning—be similar if not more grievous to us who are "grafted in" (Rom. 11:17–25)?

An important question, then, haunts us (or at least hovers over us) today. What is *our* generation? Or perhaps better stated, where does our generation fit in the greater panoply of God's purposes and prophecy? This question should grip our souls amid the most fatherless generation in memory, if not in all history. Might our plague of fatherlessness in this generation reflect our rejection of the Father and His ways since the rebirth of Israel? Might the cataclysmic war against fathers be manifesting itself in the multiplied chaos shredding the fabric of our families and cauterizing the hearts of our children?

Might our plague of fatherlessness in this generation reflect our rejection of the Father

---

"IF I BE A FATHER . . . ?"

A father yearns to be honored . . . to be respected . . . to be obeyed out of filial love and loyalty. It is not pride but a profound, inbred sense of purpose and position that calls forth a father's honor. And God the Father is no different.

"If then I be a father," He lamented, "where is mine honour? And if I be a master, where is my fear?" Not only Israel but also her spiritual leaders, the priests, had perverted God's house, provoking the Father's heart, such that they "despise my name," said the Father (Mal. 1:6). So great was the Father's sense of rejection that He declared, "I have no pleasure in you . . . neither will I accept an offering at your hand" (Mal. 1:10).

Malachi, prophetically translating the profound nature of God's broken . . . and now angry . . . father's heart, accused the pastors/priests of corrupting God's covenant by refusing or refraining from teaching the fullness of God's truth to the people, causing them to stumble in the ways of Father's house. He said, "Ye have not kept my ways, but have been partial in the law" (Mal. 2:7–9). They pandered to the people for their favor rather than faithfully proclaiming the whole counsel of God. They elevated feelings over faith, crying to God to deliver them from the consequences of their rebellious rejection of God's ways while refusing to repent of their rejection of the Father's household ways.

"And this have ye done again," saith the Lord, "covering the altar of the LORD with tears, with weeping, and crying out, insomuch that he regardeth not the offering any more, or receiveth it with good will at your hand" (Mal. 2:13).

Try to imagine the gravity of the Father's grief. So great was His grief that His favor and mercy were cut off and no longer available or extended to the very people who yet claimed entitlement to the blessings of His covenant. They pridefully persisted in claiming the Father's name yet provoked Him by perverting His ways and defying His desires.

Try to imagine the gravity of the Father's grief.

"RETURN UNTO ME"

A father yearns for his errant sons and daughters to return to the family fold. He desires not only that they bear his name but that they embrace his will and the ways of his household. And so it is with God.

God may woo and even warn His wayward children, but it is they who must return. "Return unto me," saith the Lord, "and I will return unto you." Yet shockingly the children have so seared their minds and hearts in stubborn pride that they do not comprehend the severity of the relational fracture with their Father. And so they respond with incredulity . . . "Wherein shall we return" (Mal. 3:7)?

In modern parlance, Israel and her spiritual leaders "just didn't get it." They could not . . . or would not . . . fathom that their professed faith was but an empty shell. Years and even generations of those who were purportedly "heirs according to the promise" to Abraham, having abandoned the "fear of the Lord," now waltzed in the ways of the deceiver—as Jesus noted, their "father the devil"—and judgment awaited at the door (Mal. 3:5; John 8:44).

Yeshua the Messiah, who said, "He that hath seen me hath seen the Father" (John 14:9), rebuked Israel and her spiritual leaders as "hypocrites," for He chastised, "This people honoureth me with their lips, but their heart is far from me. . . . Ye reject the commandment of God [the Father] that ye may keep your own tradition . . . making the word of God of none effect through your tradition [teachings]" (Mark 7:6–7, 9, 13; see Isa. 29:13). Yet the Father calls, "Return unto me."

The Father calls, "Return unto me."

HOW SHALL WE RETURN?

"Wherein shall we return?" asked Israel and her pastor/priests in seeming utter surprise. But the Father was quick and clear. Dare we hear His indictment of those who purported to bear the Father's name to the nations?

"You neither fear Me as God nor respect and honour Me as Father" (see Mal. 1:6; 3:5).

"You have corrupted My covenant and My house" (see Mal. 1:7–10, 14).

"You have despised My name" (see Mal. 1:6).

"You have refused to teach the fullness of My words" (see Mal. 2:7–9).

"You have dealt treacherously with your spouses, divorcing and remarrying, when I said I hate divorce and have bound you together for life" (see Mal. 2:13–16).

"You have wearied Me with your words" (see Mal. 2:17a).

"You have called what I hate 'good'" (see Mal. 2:17b).

"You even delight and bless those who refuse to obey me, fostering insurrection in My house" (see Mal. 2:17c).

"You have cavalierly disregarded My authority in My own household, supposing I will not judge you" (see Mal. 2:17d).

"You refuse to trust me, even with the tithe, which belongs to Me" (see Mal. 3:8–12).

"Your words have been stout against Me, yet you claim they have not. But you have, by rejecting My Word, My Will, and My Ways, proved your true belief that there is no value in obeying Me" (see Mal. 3:13).

"You rejoice in your rebellion, thinking that because the majority of those who claim my name are in agreement with you, professing to be 'happy', that I neither care nor will respond" (Mal. 3:15a).

"And to top it off, you tempt me beyond measure by raising the proponents of such rebellion to positions of leadership, falsely believing that they are getting away with it!" (see Mal. 3:15b).

I must remind you, said the Lord, that I the Lord keep a "book of remembrance" for those who truly fear Me as God and honor Me as Father (Mal. 3:16), "For them that honour me I will honour, and they that despise me shall be lightly esteemed" (1 Sam. 2:30).

And today, the Father's heart is deeply broken, with devastating consequences for us on the near edge of His Son's Second Coming—unless we humbly return to Him.

PROBING OUR HEARTS

1. Why would God the Father be grieved with us, with me, as a father?

2. In what ways has our generation rebelled against the Word, Will, and Ways of the Father?

3. How and why have professing Christians seemed to progressively rebel against and wander from the ways of the Father's household as defined by the Father's own Word?

4. Try to describe how the children of Israel, including their spiritual leaders, could, with straight faces, ask, "Wherein shall we return?" (Mal. 3:7) when the Father wooed and warned them, "Return unto me."

5. Do you think your name, as a father, would be in the Father's *book of remembrance* for those who truly fear God and honor Him as Father (Mal. 3:16)?

4

THE POWER OF FATHERHOOD

A good father is one of the most unsung, unpraised, unnoticed, and yet one of the most valuable assets in our society.

—BILLY GRAHAM

FATHERS ARE EITHER FAMOUS OR INFAMOUS, to one degree or another. A father is either a *father*, or he is not. A sperm donor may sow the seed for a child's life, but a father injects social and spiritual direction for the child's living and destiny.

There is no substitute for a genuine *father*. And perhaps shockingly, the very future is at stake . . . the future of our families, our society, our churches, and our nation. Yet even more solemnly, the spiritual destiny of untold millions is at risk due to fatherlessness. And God cares. He cares more deeply than we can fully comprehend.

THE ASSAULT ON YOUR LEGACY

Make no mistake. Whether or not you, I, or we are aware of it, there is a massive assault being waged against fathers and fathering. You, your legacy as a father, and the eternal destiny of your family are destined for destruction and discard in the dustbin of history.

The modern attack on fathers began with the craven, Godless rebellion of the French Revolution, which determined to destroy all earthly authority, beginning with faith and family. Chaos was the immediate and enduring consequence. Its corruption has now metastasized like an aggressive cancer throughout the Western world, leaving devastating carnage in its wake.

Then came Darwin and the theoretical corruption of God's creative purpose and order, undermining both faith and family and the eternal purpose of God-ordained fatherhood. Marx, Hegel and Freud followed, with political, social and economic and sexual theories further calculated to destroy the future of family and fathers. As we progressively abandoned the powerful reality of the Fatherhood of God, we have found our own power and purpose as earthly fathers to be profoundly diminished and on the threshold of destruction.

How, then, can this God-ordained power and purpose be recovered? The answer rests with every man and requires immediate response, for the hour is late and the culmination of history and prophecy lie straight ahead.

RE-EMBRACING FATHERLY POWER

The effective power of a father, or of fathers in general, is directly related to his perceived authority as a father in his own household. And such authority is gained, or lost, in many ways.

Authority is often gained or attributed by position. And so we might protest, "I am the father in this house." Such a protestation of "right" to authority may be ever so true by reason of position, but it may not be persuasive to effect enduring fatherly purpose.

Another means of gaining authority is by usurpation. Seldom does a man gain fatherly authority in his own household by usurpation because he has the God-given position of authority. Yet a man often loses authority in the home by a wife's usurpation of his authority, either in whole or in part. The root of this competition for authority is clearly stated as a painful consequence of the curse of the fall of man in the Garden of Eden (Gen. 3:16). Many men, however, abandon their authority by refusing to exercise it, thus leaving a mother with the unenviable task of trying to fill the father's shoes.

The third, and most powerful, means of gaining authority is by delegation, where authority is conferred upon the father by one in greater authority. It is this conferred or delegated authority that births the vision of legacy and breathes life into the father's life both to will and to do of God's good pleasure. For it is God, as Father, who confers upon men His mantle of fatherly mission. If a man fails or refuses to embrace the mantle, he will never fulfill his true fatherly mission and will leave a lamentable legacy.

How, then, can a man begin to embrace, or re-embrace such a fatherly vision where true and biblical authority is both perceived and received?

LIKE FATHER, LIKE SON

The power of fatherhood is rooted in the essential characteristics of fatherhood or in what it means, from God's perspective, to be a father. We gain our true perspective for earthly fathering from God's perspective. If our perspective differs from or diminishes God's perspective, our power as fathers will also be diminished and our longed-for legacy will languish.

Before we explore these many essential fathering characteristics, there is a fundamental prerequisite . . . so simple, yet profound:

TO BE A FATHER, YOU MUST FIRST BECOME A SON.
We see this clearly in the natural world, but our ultimate and enduring legacy will be in the spiritual realm. A rhetorical question is therefore necessary: "Am I living as a true son of God?" For if I am to be and become a good and godly father, I must first be a good and godly son, both to my earthly father and to God as my heavenly Father. Where either of those relationships is defective, my own fathering will be impaired at best or hypocritical at worst. I must set my own fathering house and heart in order if I am to be perceived as having legitimate godly authority in my home with my children, grandchildren and wife. This becomes God's *affirmative action* program to set the stage for His blessing.

For if I am to be and become a godly father, I must first be a godly son.

We can now take a brief look at the fathering essentials displayed and declared by God the Father. This will establish the foundation upon which the Lord can begin to turn our hearts to our children and our children's hearts toward us.

FOUNDATIONAL ESSENTIALS OF FATHERHOOD

Fatherhood is the overall spirit and sphere of what it means to truly be a father. This overarching concept of being a father encompasses many components. If and when any component of fatherhood is diminished or meets its demise, a father loses both authority and influence. And to the extent these fatherhood characteristics are individually or collectively ignored, spurned, or minimized, a man's legacy will be either compromised, at best, or corrupted and catastrophic at its end. Since few men desire a lamentable legacy, these foundational blocks of fatherhood are not merely important but of absolute necessity for building a good and godly legacy that lasts.

1. PURPOSE

God has ordained fatherhood for a *purpose*. That purpose is to fulfill His purpose for leadership, first with a man's wife, then with his own immediate family, continuing then to his extended family and ultimately to his broader fathering influence in the surrounding society and especially in the community of faith.

Abraham is the express example of God's purpose in fatherhood. While not perfect, he pleased God and continually pressed toward the mark, becoming the model of purposed Divine influence. It is little wonder that Abraham is referred to by both Jew and Christian believers as "the father of the faith."

Consider Abraham's calling. He was called to leave his father's home so that God could separate him for greater purpose and influence. The Lord then said, "I will make of thee a great nation, and I will bless thee . . . and thou shalt be a blessing." And in a declaration of greater—yes, grand purpose—God decreed a legacy of unimaginable proportion: "...and in thee shall all the families of the earth be blessed" (Gen. 12:1–3).

Even so must every man come to a genuine sense of God's purpose, embracing His promise by faith, and daily doing His will with expectation that through simple obedience, God will, by His gracious favor, yield a legacy above and beyond all that he can ask or ever think (Phil. 2:13; Eph. 3:20).

2. PERSPECTIVE

Fathers are ordained by God to bring His fathering perspective to earth. It is therefore no mystery why fathers and fathering have been under such enormous and increasing attack for the past three centuries. The archenemy of our souls and our society has determined to destroy or defame not only fathers and fatherhood in general but our appreciation and understanding of God as *Father*.

The assault against fatherhood and all things masculine has progressively undermined the enduring strength of true faith, replacing living *faith* with the lordship of *feelings*. The echoing consequences of this demonic sleight of hand have saturated every aspect of our culture and have invaded our churches and ministries.

The divinely ordained male perspective has been mocked and massaged into mush, emasculating the gospel and redefining God solely by a feminine mystique. Our sons and daughters desperately need both fathers and mothers, each reflecting their own aspect of the nature of God.

Perspective is similar in nature to vision, and without vision and fatherly perspective, the greater glory and purpose is either lost or languishes. *Viewpoint determines destiny!* And without a full-bodied fatherly viewpoint, destiny is either impaired or impoverished.

3. PRESENCE

There is no substitute for fatherly *presence*. Without presence, purpose wanes and perspective is lost. Presence separates mere men from manly fathers who desire their existence to have meaning.

There is no substitute for fatherly presence.

We sing of the heavenly Father, "O the glory of Your presence . . . ." The Psalmist exulted, "in thy presence is fulness of joy," for it is in His Fatherly presence He "will show me the path of life" (Ps. 16:11). Moses cried out to God, "If thy presence go not with me . . ." [I cannot provide the fatherly leadership you require of me with these children of Israel] (Ex. 33:15). Jesus, who declared, "I and my Father are one (John 10:30)," "ordained twelve, that they should be *with* him, and that he might send them forth" (Mark 3:14). True discipleship is spiritual fathering. And fathering without *withness* and *presence* is folly.

4. PRINCIPLE

Principle is the backbone of fatherhood. When pragmatism rules over principle in a man's life, he castrates himself spiritually and renders himself a eunuch, unable to bear spiritual children, let alone disciple them. He may gain a following but disconnects himself from fatherhood. This is the sad state of many men and much ministry.

A principled man is powerful in influence because he is a lover of truth. He is not swayed by the seductive dictates of culture, the mind of the seeming majority, or every wind of spiritual titillation. Neither does he vacillate under the tyrannical lordship of fleeting feelings. "His heart is fixed, trusting in the LORD" (Ps. 112:7).

5. PROTECTION

Fatherhood provides an umbrella of *protection*. It is genuine protection that can be trusted in times of trouble as well as in good times. It is reliable security that engenders faith rather than exposing to ungodly fear.

A father's protection is both practical and spiritual. He will not knowingly or negligently place those under his covering in harm's way physically, emotionally, economically, relationally or mentally. A true father sees beyond today so that those under his wing can rejoice in a godly tomorrow. While desiring happiness, he pursues holiness, ensuring God's honor, for it is written, "… them that honor me I will honour" (1 Sam. 2:30).

God's protection is secured by our trust and obedience. "Whoso putteth his trust in the LORD shall be safe," wrote Solomon (Prov. 29:25). A father's protection of his own child is secured the same way. "Honor thy father… that it may go well with thee," we read in Ephesians 6:2-3. A man whose children are disobedient will have a hard time protecting them.

6. PROVISION

Provision, at all levels, is fundamental to fatherhood. Purported protection without *provision* is perversion of God's purpose for fatherhood.

So clearly linked is provision to Divine purpose for fatherhood that the very self-described character of God is that of a provider: "Jehovah Jireh," the "God who sees and provides" (see Gen. 22:1–14). It should come as no surprise, then, that even New Testament scripture warns, "If any provide not for his own, and [e]specially those of his own house, he hath denied the faith, and is worse than an infidel" (1 Tim. 5:8).

Indeed, perhaps God's greatest fatherly lament is connected to the children of Israel's failure to value and trust their Father's provision and promise. The Father of Abraham, Isaac and Jacob cried out in pathetic pity:

> I am the LORD thy God, which brought thee out of the land of Egypt: open thy mouth wide and I will fill it.

> But my people would not hearken to my voice; and Israel would [have] none of me. . . .

> Oh that my people had hearkened unto me . . .

> [I] should have fed them also with the finest of the wheat: and with honey out of the rock should I have satisfied thee. (Ps. 81:10–16)

7. PASSION

It takes *passion* to fulfill purpose. Only godly passion born of godly purpose can fulfill the godly future of fatherhood.

Lack of godly passion for fatherhood reveals lack of godly

purpose. And absence of a profound sense of godly purpose prevents godly influence and perverts any hoped-for godly legacy that will last.

God yearns to be known and loved as "*our Father*" with all of the passion and purpose He connects with the calling of fatherhood (Matt. 6:9). He laments deeply for those who are fatherless, embracing them as their Father, knowing full well that to be fatherless is to lack a quintessential component for a purposeful and prosperous life (Ps. 68:5). Indeed Christ, in His consummate embrace of the cross in crucifixion, expressed the Father's undying passion for pitiable lost children, causing the prophet to identify the Redeemer as "the everlasting Father" (Isa. 9:6).

Lack of godly passion for fatherhood reveals lack of godly purpose.

A father without godly passion for fatherhood is nothing but a child in a man's body, adolescent in mind and selfish in spirit, living in the myopia of his eternal SELF, without vision or consciousness of divine destiny, either for himself or for his progeny.

8. PERSISTENCE

A true father is *persistent* in passion for his progeny. He is convinced that "love never fails" (1 Cor. 13:8 AMPC). He constantly "press[es] toward the mark for the prize of the high calling of God in Christ Jesus" for the fruit of God-ordained fatherhood (Phil. 3:14). While realizing he has not arrived as a perfect father, he refuses to become paralyzed by past failures and presses ever more passionately to fulfill his holy purpose as a father (see Phil. 3:13).

The persistent and passionate father realizes that his success is rooted in a divine partnership. While giving with gusto, his heart is continually full of gratitude, for he is ever conscious that "it is God which worketh in [him] both to will and to do of his good pleasure" (Phil. 2:13). He fathers faithfully, without murmuring or complaining, realizing he is in partnership with the heavenly Father, who, in his express person in Jesus Christ, is full of both grace and truth (Phil. 2:14; John 1:14).

The persistent father seeks faithfully to be blameless, as a son of God the Father, in the midst even of a crooked and perverse generation, shining as a light, holding forth the word of truth and life, that he may rejoice at the coming of the Lord, knowing that his fatherhood and his labors have not been in vain (Phil. 2:15–16).

9. PATIENCE

Patience is divine elasticity, enabling the process of fathering to fulfill God's promise without fracturing the brittle bones of often recalcitrant sons and daughters. Similarly, impatience frustrates the enabling grace of God, short-circuiting God's long-suffering as our Father.

Well knowing our own imperfection despite our holy passion for fathering, patience paves the way for our persistence in purpose to pay off, in the end, to God's glory and to our joy. Impatience can, and often does, destroy the work both we and God have been doing in the nurture of immature sons, daughters and disciples and can severely impact our own relationship with our long-suffering Father.

The trying of our fatherly faith works patience, and we must let patience have its perfect work that we, as fathers, may be complete, lacking in nothing (Jas. 1:3–4).

10. PRAYERFULNESS

Prayerfulness is the attitude of continual submission between fathers on earth and the heavenly Father, who changes not. Without continual prayer, a father is on his own . . . a very lonely place indeed.

We fathers need a Father who provides fatherly wisdom and does not criticize us for seeking it. Rather, our heavenly Father rejoices in our seeking Him and His wisdom with a whole heart:

> And ye shall seek me, and find me, when ye shall search for me with all your heart. And I will be found of you, saith the LORD. . . .
>
> Then shall ye call upon me, and ye shall go and pray unto me, and I will hearken unto you. . . .
>
> For I know the thoughts that I think toward you, saith the LORD, thoughts of peace, and not of evil, to give you an expected end [NKJV: a future and a hope]. (Jer. 29:13–14, 12, 11)

Yet let no man claim prayerful connectedness with the Father for his own fathering if he comes with unclean hands or an impure heart, for he shall be disconnected from the favor and blessing of the Lord (see Ps. 24:4–5). Repent, return and rejoice in the favor of your Father.

11. PROMISE

A father's purpose is translated into true fatherhood through the father's *promise*. Without promise, both toward sons and daughters and toward fathers, purpose becomes little more than unfounded hope. Such hope is so perpetually deferred that it makes the heart sick, sucking the substance out of relational fatherhood (Prov. 13:12).

Fatherhood, by its very nature, implies promise to those under its fathering wings. The *wings* are metaphorical for a promise of covering, protection and provision—in other words . . . an overarching promise. "Therefore," rejoiced the psalmist, "the children of men put their trust under the shadow of thy wings" (Ps. 36:7).

A true father's greatest desire is the loving trust of his children. Yet there is no trust without either express or implied promise. When either express or implied promise by a father is broken, trust is fractured, godly influence wanes, and legacy looms as a painful liability.

> Cast not away therefore your confidence. . . . For you have need of patience, that after ye have done the will of God, ye might receive the *promise*. (Heb. 10:35–36)

12. POWER

Fatherhood, by its very nature derived from God's Fatherhood, has *power*. Yet we are admonished that in any governmental system, "power tends to corrupt and absolute power corrupts absolutely." How then are we as earthly fathers to handle such delegated power or authority without corrupting it into a diabolical dictatorship?

A true father's greatest desire is the loving trust of his children.

The answer is in simple submission, always in an attitude of surrender to the Father's will. As it is written, even Jesus, the only begotten Son of God, "being found in fashion as a man, humbled himself, and became obedient." Because of this willingness to humble Himself, "God . . . highly exalted him (Phil. 2:8, 9)." Even so is our own fatherhood exalted, birthing godly influence and an eternal kingdom legacy.

Yet more power remains. It is not the power from delegated authority but from Divine *dunamis* . . . the Holy Spirit. This is the power of a Fathering promise. As Jesus, Son of the Father, declared to the disciples He had fathered: "wait for the promise of the Father" (Acts 1:4). And, "Behold, I send the promise of my Father upon you . . . until ye be endued with power from on high" (Luke 24:49).

It is both delegated and *dunamis* power that every father needs to define godly destiny, both for natural and spiritual children, and to display godly power, that we might confidently leave a legacy that will last for eternity.

PROBING OUR HEARTS

1. Why might the devil, the arch-deceiver, have destined to leave fatherhood discarded "in the dustbin of history"?

2. What social scientific, economic and spiritual forces have combined to destroy true fatherhood?

3. What is the most powerful means of gaining and sustaining true fatherly authority?

4. Have you considered why, in order "to be a father, you must first become a son"? What do you think is the Father's current viewpoint toward your life as a "son"?

5. What two forms of power does a father need to confidently leave a godly legacy?

5

THE CURSE OF FATHERLESSNESS

Fathering can be a lonely job. The cost of failing is so high that it could be disastrous.

—DAN SEABORN, *PARENTING WITH GRACE AND TRUTH*

THE ABSENCE OF FATHERS is a premier sign of God's absence in any generation and of God's rejection in our generation . . . these latter days of human history. And the reason is not a mystery.

THE MYSTERY OF FATHERHOOD

Mysteries are not always as mysterious as they might initially appear on the surface. In reality, the very framing of something as a *mystery* is often a call to discern and discover that which may not be immediately apparent to the casual observer. Hence, "the mystery of the kingdom of God" (Mark 4:11), "the mystery of his will" (Eph. 1:9), "the mystery of Christ" (Eph. 3:4), "the mystery of the gospel" (Eph. 6:19), "the mystery of godliness" (1 Tim. 3:16) and "the mystery of iniquity" (2 Thess. 2:7) are all *mysteriously* brought to our mystery-loving attention by God as Father.

Perhaps surprisingly, the word *mystery* or *mysteries* occurs no fewer than twenty-eight times in the Bible, all in the New Testament. But perhaps the greatest of all *mysteries* to modern man is the seeming mystery of the fatherhood of God and its profound implications, both spiritually and even secularly for earthbound society. Whether God as *Father* is seen as mystery or metaphor, the message is momentous for all of us on the near edge of the Second Coming of God's "only begotten Son," the Messiah.

MASKING THE MYSTERY

A mystery remains mysterious to the extent that it is either unknown or shrouded in the fog of unperceived obstacles that frustrate or mask the knowability or discernability of the mystery by casually-minded men. This is the moral and spiritual environment amid which the deceiver, who rages in jealousy over the Fatherhood of God, achieves his pernicious plans to emasculate the perceived Fatherhood of God by demasculinizing the planet, exalting the feminine to be worshipped.

Thus, the very concept of God as Father is and has been corrupted throughout history. Notably, nearly all pagan religion has worshipped the feminine from antiquity, finding its root in the consequences of mankind's fall (Gen. 3:16). From Babylon to Persia, from Persia to Greece, and from Greece to Rome the pattern persists, even to the popes leading purported *Christian* congregants in worship of "the Queen of Heaven."

The very concept of God as Father is and has been corrupted throughout history.

It is precisely this alternative and corrupt view of creation and authority, and the resulting shift of adoration that persistently brought God's passion against both Israel and Judah (Jer. 44:17–25), causing God to lament, "if . . . I be a father, where is mine honour?" (Mal. 1:6). Feminine feelings had become lord, and God the Father had become nothing but a mascot. The mystery was masked. Father was forsaken.

UNMASKING THE MYSTERY

If, indeed, as many are increasingly convinced, we are living in times known not only as *the last days*, which began at Pentecost(Acts 2:16–19), but also in *the end of the age* or *the latter years* (Ezek. 38:8), *the latter days* (Ezek. 38:16), *the latter time* (Dan. 8:23), *the end of the world* (Matt. 24:3), *the day of the* Lord (Joel 1:15; 2:1; Amos 5:18; Zeph. 1:14) or *the day of his wrath* (Rev. 6:17), it should be well understood that the enemy of our souls is intensifying his violent and virulent efforts to forever destroy the *Fatherhood of God* in the estimation of God's people and the entire planet.

This nefarious and deadly deception must be unmasked and the truth must be restored in our time. The need is urgent and the call is without compromise. Either God will be *Father*, or He will not. It is a matter of the heart, and destiny for many rides in the balance.

It is for this eternal reason that God, in a final expression of His mercy, compassion, and grace, is now calling "the heart of the fathers to the children, and the heart of the children to the fathers" (Mal. 4:5–9). Fathers on earth are to practically and prophetically model the heart of the heavenly Father, thus revealing the holy mystery of the Father's heart, drawing all who will hear and heed to the Father's eternal home, where loving and faithful obedience is the calling card, revealing genuine trust and faith, just as Jesus exemplified for us all. As it is written:

> Though he were a Son, yet learned he obedience by the things which he suffered; and being made perfect, he became the author of eternal salvation *unto all them that obey him*. (Heb. 5:8–9)

Therefore,

> Let this mind be in you, which was also in Christ Jesus . . . And being found in fashion as a man, *he humbled himself and became obedient* unto death, even the death of the cross. Wherefore God hath highly exalted him . . .
>
> Wherefore, my beloved as ye have always obeyed [have we?] . . . work out your own salvation with fear and trembling.
>
> For it is God [the Father] which worketh in you both to will and to do of his good pleasure. (Phil. 2:5–13)

THE DESPISED "FOUR-LETTER WORD"

It is fascinating, but pervasively true. The most hated word among professing Christians in the Western world today is the little word *obey*. It has for all spiritual purposes become, as it were, a *four-letter word*, to be skirted, avoided or derided. Yet it is the *only* word in Scripture that defines, in the most fundamental way, that which pleases God as Father.

Fathers on earth are to practically and prophetically model the heart of the heavenly Father.

In a very simple yet substantive way, to despise and distance ourselves from the very word *obey* is to distance ourselves from our heavenly Father, effectively declaring ourselves *fatherless*. We then cast ourselves upon the collective wisdom (or ignorance) of the children, rising in democratic defiance against the Father's household of true faith as defined exclusively by the Father's Word.

This perhaps unwitting defiance now defines the life and ways of the American and Western church, from pulpit to pew, and the picture, from the Father's viewpoint, is not pretty.

Thus, professing Christians have little, if any, persuasive or prophetic authority in the broader culture, for we ourselves are not truly under authority . . . and the pagan culture well knows it. We formerly sang "Trust and Obey." We now purport to *trust* without *obedience*.

As *Time* presciently and perhaps prophetically warned us on April 5, 1993, we have created "a custom-made God, one made in our own image."[1]

A CULTURE OF FATHERLESSNESS

Fatherlessness now, and for the past generation, defines American life and culture . . . indeed, the culture of the entire Western ("Christian") world. The aftershock of the tectonic shaking rooted in the collective rebellion of the 1960s and its sexual revolution have nearly demolished the last vestiges of the Father's apparent governance both in the culture and in the church.

Fatherlessness now defines American life and culture.

It is well known but seldom discussed, whether in the church house or the White House, that fatherlessness lies at the root of nearly all of the most glaring problems that plague our modern, now post-Christian life. The greatest sources of economic upheaval—specifically, poverty—are unwed childbirth and divorce, each of which is government-sponsored fatherlessness in the name of humanistic *compassion*.

From such false compassion, the welfare system was born and 70 percent of the children in our inner cities are born without fathers to whom their mothers are married. Eighty-five percent of those same children live in homes without their fathers. And perhaps shockingly, well over 40 percent of all American children are born to mothers who are not married to their fathers, and over 50 percent of all men and women now cohabit rather than marry.

THE CURSE OF FATHERLESSNESS

The *curse* described by the prophet Malachi (4:6) is not only upon us but is decimating what was once known and even honored as a *Christian* nation. The glory of God once displayed from "the land of the free" has been disgraced, leaving the "home of the brave" lamenting over the violence that terrorizes our streets and fills our prisons.

Indeed, the curse is not coming but is now culminating in overwhelming waves and could well metastasize into martial law, removing all conditionally *guaranteed* freedoms.

The primary fault and fault lines lie not with the politicians but rather with pastors and parachurch leaders who, for the last two or three generations, have progressively determined to please the culture rather than Christ, who was sent by the Father, who demands obedience. The dissing of obedience in the name of "mercy, grace and compassion" has now brought the curse of fatherlessness upon us. And no amount of spiritualized rationalization can either relieve us of responsibility or reprieve the mushrooming consequential curse.

The only remedy is repentance.

PROBING OUR HEARTS

1. Why might the absence of true fathers be "a premier sign of God's absence" in our generation or in any generation?

2. In what ways has the very concept of God as Father been corrupted by the deceiver throughout history? Do you see it even in our churches?

3. Is it true, in a very real sense, that whether "God will be Father" is actually a matter of my heart? Why might that be?

4. How has false compassion led to a culture of fatherlessness?

5. Why is it that when we distance ourselves from the word *obey*, we also distance ourselves from the Father?

6

NO SONS, NO FATHERS

Too many fathers—even those in leadership—have spiritual lives akin to the old commercials for Brylcreem, the hairstyling gel: "A little dab'll do ya."

—SOURCE UNKNOWN

WITHOUT FATHERS, WE HAVE NO SONS. This is true both in the natural and in the spiritual realms. The spiritual metaphor based on the natural concept of *father* is woven throughout Scripture, in both Old and New Testaments. Destiny is largely dependent upon embracing this elementary principle.

OBEDIENCE IS THE KEY
Children are enjoined by God as Father to "obey your parents in the Lord: for this is right" (Eph. 6:1). Why is this *right*? It is because the earthly father stands in for and represents the

heavenly Father's prescribed line of both authority and awesome respect.

For this reason, the heavenly Father requires children to "honor [their] father and mother; which is the first commandment with promise; that it may be well with [them], and that [they] may live long on the earth" (Eph. 6:2–3; Ex. 20:12). But what happens when children are either deprived of the legitimate father relationship or are determined to rebel against it? The curse comes, first gradually, seemingly imperceptibly, until the spirit of such fractured fatherhood gains progressive cultural dominion, breeding consequential destruction.

Fathers also have an ever-greater responsibility in the relationship than do the children. Remember, it is the father who stands, as it were, in the place of God. And there could hardly be a greater or graver responsibility or calling. For this reason, we fathers are forewarned to treat our children accordingly, properly disciplining and correcting them, but not "provok[ing our] children to wrath" (Eph. 6:4), which provocation may turn the child against not only the earthly father but against God as Father. Have we not heard multiplied such painful testimonies over the last several generations as godly fatherhood has degenerated?

A SIGN OF THE TIMES

Have we not, for at least three generations, been experiencing before our very eyes this seldom-referenced or understood "sign of the times" or of the "end of the age"? Is this not what the prophet Malachi specifically addressed and foretold would take place immediately preceding "the coming of the great and dreadful day of the Lord" (Mal. 4:5)?

Is it any wonder that the great Father heart of God would in these last days—these latter days of world history—make a final and eternally echoing plea, heard both in heaven and on earth, that the hearts of fathers be restored and the hearts of children be revived, all through the amazing *grace* of fatherhood? Why would we resist such divine passion? Would we stubbornly straight-arm such a divine plan and purpose? The annals of prophetic history will reveal our answer and its consequences, whether for calamity or for the outflow of blessing from corrective righteousness. No father is exempted.

THE NATURAL AND THE SPIRITUAL

As with *natural* fatherhood, so it is and will be with *spiritual* fatherhood. From God's viewpoint as Father, they are inextricably linked. A natural father is expected by God to not only fulfill his duty and calling to provide all of the accoutrements of earthly fatherhood but to also fulfill his responsibility to provide faithful spiritual leadership (fatherhood), both by precept and example.

Consider Jesus, the "only begotten Son of God." The Father declared, "I will be to him a Father, and he shall be to me a Son" (Heb. 1:5). Similarly, God (as Father), urges us to leave the household of Satan and his ways so that God's Fatherhood will be honored and that we might be blessed.

> Wherefore come out from among them [the world and its culture], and be ye separate, saith the Lord, . . . and I will receive you. And will be a Father unto you, and ye shall be my sons and daughters, saith the Lord Almighty. (see 2 Cor. 6:14–18)

Abraham set an early example of spiritual fatherhood both by precept and example, becoming the "father of all them that believe" (Rom. 4:11). Because of his faith and faith-*full* life, it was promised that "he should be the heir of the world" (Rom. 4:13). Consider well the implications for those who will truly and righteously follow in his fatherly steps. Abraham was given inheritance and a legacy because he, as a son, *obeyed* the Father, looking "for a city which hath foundations, whose builder and maker is God" (Heb. 11:8–10).

Jesus also, as the Son of the Father and as the son of Abraham, inherited all things because He *obeyed* the Father (Phil. 2:8–11). We, then, as obedient sons, are to "work out our own salvation [as fathers] with fear and trembling," knowing confidently that "it is God [the Father] which worketh in you both to will and to do of his good pleasure" (Phil. 2:12–13).

BECOMING A "FATHER"

Perhaps the most quintessential truth underlying genuine fatherhood is one we discussed earlier. It is simply this . . .

To become a father,

I must first become a son.

This truth, at first glance, may seem strange. On the other hand, it may seem so elementary as to be unworthy of additional discussion. But let's explore it a bit further. From a biblical or spiritual viewpoint, it is one of the simplest yet most profound truths of the Bible. And our failure or refusal to grasp its significance and personally embrace it has led to immeasurable pain, frustration, and even destruction.

From a natural perspective, that being sons precedes our physical ability to become fathers is a given, required of the natural order of life. Yet for some reason, this same obvious fact seems to escape significance for many if not most in the spiritual realm. But if we who profess salvation in Christ are to truly become spiritual fathers, we must deeply embrace and comprehend both the fact and functional reality of *sonship*.

It is interesting that the most common reference to men in Scripture is not as *father* but rather as *son*. We are given power or authority to "become the sons of God" (John 1:12). "As many as are led by the Spirit of God," wrote the apostle Paul, "they are the sons of God" (Rom. 8:14).

What happens if we profess faith in Christ yet refuse to walk in His authority? What conclusions are to be drawn for a man who professes salvation in Christ yet refuses to walk according to the Spirit of Christ? It is the life answers to these elementary questions that reflect whether we are truly *sons* of God . . . and if we are not truly *sons* but pretenders, how then can we hope to become spiritual fathers?

If we are not truly sons but pretenders, how then can we hope to become spiritual fathers?

It is said, and rightly so, that "Jesus paid it all," but He also, in *paying it all*, as a son, displayed for all time what it looks like to truly be a *son* who could fulfill the Father's will "in bringing many sons unto glory" (Heb. 2:10). Absolute humble obedience to Father's Word and obedience to the Spirit of Truth confirmed Jesus' sonship (Phil. 2:7–11).

This same humble obedience will confirm our sonship as well, laying the necessary life foundation for genuine spiritual fatherhood.

> That ye may be blameless and harmless, the sons of God, without rebuke, in the midst of a crooked and perverse nation; among whom ye shine as lights in the world. (Phil. 2:15)

Remember well! To become a *father*, I must first become a *son*. Without true fathers, there will be no true sons. What a joyous and enormously fulfilling opportunity and challenge we have to walk in the authority of God's sons, obedient even to the death of our fleshly natures, walking humbly, yet boldly, in His Spirit.

LAST OF ALL

"But last of all [the Father] sent unto them his son, saying, They will reverence my son" (Matt. 21:37). Yet most did not. Even the most seemingly religious rejected the true Son because He lived and spoke with obedient consistency according to the Father's will (John 5:42–44). "But as many as received him, to them gave he power [i.e. authority] to become the sons of God [the Father], even to them that believe [obey out of trust and submission] on his name" (John 1:12).

Therefore, it is written, "Beloved, now are we the sons of God . . . and every man that hath this hope in him purifieth himself, even as he [the obedient Son of God] is pure. . . . "Whosoever abideth in him [the Son] sinneth not: whosoever sinneth hath not seen him, neither known him" (1 John 3: 2–3, 6).

For this reason, "God dealeth with you as with sons; for what son is he whom the Father chasteneth not? . . . Shall we not much rather be in subjection unto the Father of spirits and live" (Heb. 12:7, 9)?

As it is written, "For as many as are led by the Spirit of God [not the world and the carnal nature], they are the sons of God" through "the Spirit of adoption, whereby we cry, Abba Father" (Rom. 8:14–15).

A FEW GOOD SONS

In these ultimate, historic and prophetic times, the Father is yearning for a few good sons . . . a remnant of righteous men who can be trusted to *father* many sons into glory, as did the only begotten Son. Will the Son, in these final days of human history, be delighted . . . or ashamed . . . to call us *brethren* (Heb. 2:11)?

This is our challenge as we approach the culmination of all things. Will we courageously and faithfully take on the mantle of true sons proffered to us by the example and exhortation of the "only begotten Son" of God, or will we default, leaving the desperation of father-*less-ness* in the wake of our defeat?

The destiny of many rests in the balance of our decision. Indeed, these are "the days of Elijah." And so, the Holy Spirit warns and woos . . . "To day if ye will hear his voice, harden not your hearts" (Heb. 3:7–8). But rather, see things from the Father's viewpoint as He woos us to become sons who can be genuine spiritual fathers in what may well be the final generation of the Father's redemptive plan.

> But Christ *as a son* [was faithful] over his own house; whose house are we, *if* we hold fast the confidence and the rejoicing of the hope firm unto the end. (Heb. 3:6)

PROBING OUR HEARTS

1. In what ways does the lack of true sons reveal the lack of true fathers?

2. How is disobedience the root of false sonship, thus depriving the world of genuine fathers?

3. Can you fathom why God, as Father, would seek to warn the world—each of us—as to the curse due to the lack of genuine fathers, both natural and spiritual?

4. What is the most essential truth underlying genuine fatherhood?

5. Are there any areas of your life that either limit or perhaps even disqualify you from being one of the *few good sons* the Father yearns for in this generation?

6. Do you believe these truly are *the days of Elijah*? Why, or why not?

7

FORSAKING OUR FATHERS

By not *accepting our rank of headship "as unto the Lord," we are* beheading *our families.*
　　　　　—JAMES LANGLOIS, *THE FAMILY BIBLE REVOLUTION*

IT IS AMERICA'S HYMN. It is a hymn long sung but now long forgotten. Consider again the impassioned stanza.

Our fathers' God to Thee.

Author of liberty,

To Thee we sing;

Long may our land be bright

With freedom's holy light;

Protect us by Thy might

Great God, our King.

...re, in these beautiful words impregnated with a passion largely forgotten, are both prayer and praise for God as Father of our nation's fathers, ultimately embraced as our true King. Deep in this simple prayer resides prophetic purpose and power . . . even persuasion—that our land be seen as *bright*, that freedom's light is *holy*, and that our Father's might as both God and King will *protect* us as "author of liberty" in this divine endeavor.

Yet, lurking within these blessed lines is a prophetic burden. Unfortunately, whether or not we care to recognize it, the obverse of every promise is a potential curse. If the premise of the promise is forsaken, the future is compromised to the extent our decisions drift or deviate from the premise upon which the promise is contingent.

The premise of the hymn's promise is that God is our nation's fathers' Father and that He is both our God and King, having both the right to rule and actually reign over our land and its people. To the extent, then, that we renege, rebel or resist against those three roles of the Creator, the promised "protection by Thy might" is compromised or withdrawn.

FATHERHOOD IS THE FOUNDATION

A father seeks to bless and provide for his family. He also is committed to protect his family. But if the family, or any member of the family, resists (either in whole or in part) the father's underlying principles upon which his protection is based, the protection is reduced, minimized, or even destroyed. The father's sincere desire to bless and protect is progressively voided until no remedy remains and the carnage and chaos the father sought to protect against takes its natural course through man's carnal nature to a calamitous conclusion.

This, then, is America's current plight. The Fatherhood of God has been resisted and rejected over generations. Our fathers' God has been redefined and reconfigured into a God made in our own image. (See *Time*, April 5, 1993.) From pulpit to pew and from the church house to the White House, we have rejected, either in whole or in part, the true Fatherhood of God. So great is that rejection that Father's Word is no longer "law" even in His own household, the Church, for whom the word *obey* is a mocked "four letter word."

The rejection of God as Father has manifested itself in the progressive mocking of our earthly fathers throughout virtually all media forms. Even our churches have, either wittingly or unwittingly, joined in the fray to diminish men and undermine fathers. From the rage of feminism to the roiling embrace of divorce, fathers have effectively become persona non grata in modern American culture . . . lamentably, even in our churches . . . and this spirit of rebellion against the Creator's order has been thus exported throughout the entire Western world, insidiously infecting the entire planet.

The rejection of God as Father has manifested itself in the progressive mocking of our earthly fathers

---

THE "BRIGHT LAND" BECOMING DARK

"If . . . the light that is in thee be darkness, how great is that darkness!" declared Jesus (Matt. 6:23). But what does such *darkness* look like "on the ground"—in practical and persuasive reality? Dare we look at the painful reality that should cause any reasonable mind and heart to recoil? A brief peering into the darkness should suffice:

"Fathers disappear from households across America," reads the headline of an article in the *Washington Times*. The writer goes on to say, "The decline has hit disproportionately in the South, which considers itself a bastion of traditional values."[1]

According to the CDC, DOJ, DHHS and the Census Bureau, the 30 percent of America's children who live apart from their fathers account for

- 63 percent of teen suicides

- 70 percent of juvenile incarcerations

- 71 percent of high school dropouts

- 75 percent of children in drug abuse centers

- 86 percent of rapists

- 85 percent of youths in prison

- 85 percent of children with behavioral disorders

- 90 percent of homeless and runaway children

- 90 percent of children living in poverty

- 100 percent of gang members

In the black community, 85 percent of all children in poverty do not live in a home with their father, and 72 percent are born out of wedlock.[2] And "among the children of divorce, half have never visited their father's home," and "in a typical year 40 percent of them don't see their father."[3]

HOPE AMID HORROR

Amid such devastating and discouraging horror, is there any hope? And if so, where does that hope lie? Is there a legacy that can be recovered that will last?

Indeed there is hope, but it rests not in programs nor in glib, cheerleading *prophecies* that all will be swell . . . eventually. It should be clear that we cannot persist in current practices and the attitudes that drive them. Something must change. What must change does not and cannot begin with *them* but with *me*. Such change is and must be intensely personal. As the prophet so clearly expressed, it begins in our hearts as fathers. *Our* hearts then necessarily becomes *your* heart . . . and *mine*.

The hearts of the fathers must turn (Mal. 4:5–6). To *turn* means to profoundly change direction. Such change must not be *moderate* but *momentous*! The heart change will then produce *hope*.

So what does such heart change look like? In simple overview that we will later define with more particularity, three fundamental changes or conversions are required.

First—as men, we must recover the fullest meaning of the Fatherhood of God and its implications for our own households.

Second—as men, we must truly come to understand, in operational terms for our lives, what it means to be "sons of God."

Third—as men, we must then begin to intentionally live our lives prophetically, as living examples of the Word and will of the Lord in our daily discussions, thus imparting to our sons and daughters genuine godly destiny.

Once we catch the vision for such *prophetic* fatherhood, life will never again be the same. A new joy and sense of purpose will transform the mundane into genuine ministry with momentous implications. Time is very short, and what we do we must do quickly. As our hearts change, our homes will change, and hope will emerge from the seemingly hopeless darkness that envelops us.

Once we catch the vision for such prophetic fatherhood, life will never again be the same.

As it is written, "To day *if* you will hear His voice . . ." (Heb. 3:7, 15). We, then, as earthly fathers can and should be sons over our homes even as "Christ [is] a son over his own house." And if our hearts are truly turned in the same direction as Christ's, in obedience to the Father, we also will be able to "hold fast the confidence and the rejoicing of the hope firm unto the end" (Heb. 3:6).

PROBING OUR HEARTS

1. If God is truly our Father and we are walking and living as true sons, why is our country disintegrating into chaos and lawlessness?

2. Can you see ways in which the Fatherhood of God has been both resisted and rejected over the last several generations—even in His own house?

3. How has rejection of the Fatherhood of God undermined earthly fathers and diminished men in our generation?

4. Are you able to grasp . . . and perhaps gasp at . . . how both the absence of physical fathers and the lack of true spiritual fathers in our families have struck our country with a curse?

5. If *the hearts of the fathers* must turn, in what ways is the Father wooing you to turn . . . specifically . . . significantly?

8

CHANGING OUR WANT-TO'S

The eyes of the LORD run to and fro throughout the whole earth, to shew himself strong in the behalf of them [fathers] whose heart is perfect toward him.

—2 CHRONICLES 16:9

MY HEART DICTATES WHAT I WANT. And that is indeed dangerous if my heart is disconnected in any way from what my heavenly Father wants. It sets me at odds with Him in ways that ultimately affect not only my own destiny but also the destiny of my family and everyone within my broader sphere of influence. My *want-to's* reflect my heart and yet often repel the very ultimate blessing I so crave.

FATHERS, GRANDFATHERS AND THE FAMILY
To best understand this matter of our "want-to's," it is necessary,

or at least helpful, to open a window into our own extended family life.

My wife and I have three daughters and ten grandchildren. Four of those grandchildren have spent extended periods of their lives in our own home for convenience, giving me the unusual role of being not just a doting grandfather but also, due to proximity and ongoing presence, somewhat more of a "father," though never replacing the authority of their own father, who has always been their *father* in the home. This unusual role has served to reveal a simple yet substantive truth for all of us.

Often, especially when our grandchildren were younger, I would ask them to do various things to assist in the home or to take care of other duties, such as schoolwork. Their nearly invariable response at these early ages was, "But I don't want to." And my invariable response was, "Then change your *want-to's*." Whether we want to admit it or not, this is the condition of most *Christian* fathers today in relation to our heavenly Father.

God speaks to us. He sets forth clear and simple expectations for those who claim to be in His household. And the apostle John declared that meeting those expectations is the only way to please the Father (1 John 5:2–3). Yet we, either overtly or covertly in our hearts, respond, "But I don't want to." That is what the Bible refers to as *rebellion*. We, in whole or in part, choose to *dis*-agree with what our Father has said. We do this in many ways—sometimes subtly, yet often blatantly. Yet we expect our own sons and daughters to respect our own authority. As wrote the Psalmist, "All the foundations of the earth are out of course" (Ps. 82:5)! But "if the foundations be destroyed," he asked elsewhere, "what can the righteous do" (Ps. 11:3)?

WHAT CAN THE RIGHTEOUS DO?

Obviously, we must change our "want-to's." But how do we do that? There are seven essential steps to enable us to change our "want-to's," thus reestablishing the foundations of genuine fatherhood with our sons and daughters. Each of these steps is essential and cannot be circumvented in haste to achieve necessary change; otherwise hypocrisy will own our hearts.

1. RETURN. "Return unto me, and I will return unto you" (Mal. 3:7). This is Father God's last message to Israel before four hundred years of prophetic silence, testing His people to truly measure the genuineness of their desire and willingness to follow Him as His sons and daughters. The implication is clear. Israel, the Father's anointed and appointed (Ps. 2:2; 105:15), had strayed far from the ways of His household. The Father, brokenhearted, had lamented, "…if I be a father, where is mine honour?" (Mal. 1:6). This last message from the Father to the children of Israel before the coming of the Messiah is a fatherly rebuke and passionate plea, setting forth His viewpoint of the chosen people's long vacation from the ways of their Father's household. The consequences were palpable and proliferating: corruption of God's covenant, destruction of the covenant of marriage, moral carnage and a curse on the whole nation (Mal. 3:9), yet in their rebellion, their senses were cauterized so they either could not, or would not, hear the Father's pleading voice and broken heart.

Consider carefully their response. Does it not resemble our own today? "What have we spoken so much against thee?" they retorted (Mal. 3:13). And with a tinge of facetious sarcasm, they asked, "Wherein shall we return?" (Mal. 3:7) They had drifted so far from the spiritual security of the Father's covenantal embrace that they were adrift on the seas of moral relativity, not recognizing they were no longer under their Father's protective hand.

They had removed themselves from the Father's household while continuing to claim His name vicariously through Abraham. And the Father, longing for restoration of the protective and rejoicing relationship, stretched out His holy hand, crying "Return unto me, and I will return unto you" (Mal. 3:7).

The Father's cry then culminated with a final offer to us, in these last days . . . these latter days . . . to send a prophetic voice. That voice would seem as one "crying in the wilderness" to prepare the way of the Lord (Mal. 3:1–2; Isa. 40:3). And that final consummation of the Father's mercy, truth and grace for all history would woo and warn, seeking to "turn the heart of the fathers to the children, and the heart of the children to their fathers..." (Mal. 4:5–6). Yet before that can be accomplished, the Father requires us to "return unto" Him.

If we would truly return, we must repent.

Like ancient Israel and Judah, we also must now return. And we must return "with [our] whole heart" (Jer. 24:7), *not* continue to inquire, "Wherein shall we return?"

2. REPENT. If we would truly *return*, we must *repent*. To *repent* is both simple, and supremely difficult. Repentance is simple because it requires only that we (I) agree with Father's viewpoint or assessment of our relationship with Him. Agreement with

Father's mind and heart necessarily, and quite simply, requires a change of both attitude and corresponding action on our part so that we come into full alignment with the Word of the Father and with the ways of His household. It is a change of both mind and heart . . . exactly what we expect of our own children.

Yet that is precisely why true repentance appears so difficult . . . supremely difficult. It is the reason why our own children find it so hard to obey and stiffen themselves against parental will.

The "children of Israel," in effect, type us all as *children*. Our own want-to's continually chafe against the Father's will and often supersede it, to our shame and even separation. If the hearts of the children are to be "turned toward their father," the hearts of the fathers, as children, must be turned toward the Father, both in spirit and in truth.

If, indeed, we would return to the Father, we must first humbly repent as little children. Will pride stiffen our necks, as with the "children of Israel," or will we again, in full preparation for the return of Christ, the only fully obedient Son, humble ourselves in heartfelt obedience as did Jesus? (see Phil. 2:5-11). History and Heaven will record our answer.

3. RENEW. If the hearts of the children are to be turned back toward their fathers, the minds of the fathers must first be renewed. We fathers, as little children before our heavenly Father, must be "renewed," as the apostle Paul exhorted, "in the spirit of your mind" (Eph. 4:23).

A genuine change of attitude always reveals itself in a change of actions, where each conforms day by day to the Father's Word and ways. This is not something the Father does for us. We must be willing to "die daily" to our own will and desires

(1 Cor. 15:31) and do His pleasure instead. If we, as earthly fathers, are willing (as little children) to make the needed choices, our Father will assist us through His favor to make the needed changes.

Wherefore, you and I are exhorted first to "put off concerning the former conversation [life] the old man . . . and put on the new man . . . created in righteousness and true holiness" (Eph. 4:22–24). We are to give no place to the devil, but to be "followers of God, as dear children," walking as "children of light," having nothing to do with "the unfruitful works of darkness" (Eph. 4:27; 5:1–11).

As sons of God, we must no longer "be conformed to this world" and its life-changing culture, but rather "be transformed by the renewing of [our] mind," that we might "prove what is that good, and acceptable, and perfect, will of God [the Father]" (Rom. 12:2).

If repentance is real, we will renew ourselves daily in our Father's will and ways, that we might please Him. Then our own children will gradually be drawn back to us in repentance and restoration of relationship.

4. RIGHTEOUSNESS. Restoration of *righteousness*—or "right-ways-ness"—is the natural result of returning, repentance, and renewal of mind and heart. Righteousness and holiness are prerequisites to the Father's continuing favor, not only for individuals, but for families and nations. Righteousness either facilitates or frustrates the joy of relationship, whether with our heavenly Father or with our children.

It is little wonder, then, that righteousness is perhaps the overarching theme of Scripture, both in the Old and New

Testaments. The persistent pressure of the Father on His professed children, delivered by both prophet and apostle, was to promote righteousness in both attitude and action. This pursuit of righteousness and holiness that sets us apart from the carnal ways of the world and surrounding culture is foremost in the heart of the Father, and it must therefore be foremost in the life and living example of fathers. Only then have we any right to a legitimate expectation that our sons and daughters will follow suit.

This absolute requirement of righteousness and holiness is supremely challenging to fathers, both past and present. It is perhaps an even greater challenge to our generation because we have abandoned the "fear of the Lord" while swimming in a spiritual cesspool of multiculturalism, religious pluralism and political correctness in which the mantra of the day is "If it feels good, do it."

We have abandoned the "fear of the Lord" while swimming in a spiritual cesspool.

Consider soberly the heart of the Father in this regard. The word *righteousness* appears 308 times throughout the Bible

PROBING OUR HEARTS

1. Why are we, as fathers, so prone to say in our hearts to the Father, "But I don't want to"?

2. What is the most despised word in the church . . . and why?

3. How can we best reestablish the foundation of genuine fatherhood in the lives of our children? What is most difficult for you?

4. Why are we so prone to try to *resist the devil*, yet so resistant to *submit to God*?

5. In what ways might a revived and reverent faith in a father's life bring rejoicing in the life of the family over time?

9

THE FEAR OF THE FATHER

Blessed is the man that feareth the LORD, that delighteth greatly in His commandments.

—PSALM 112:1

FATHERLY FEAR PRECEDES FATHERLY FAITH. Fear *of* the Father precedes faith *in* the Father. This may, at first impression, be shocking to our senses given our pervasive feelings-based culture, but it remains troublingly true.

HOLY FEAR—HOLY FAITH

What the Scriptures reveal, from Genesis to Revelation, is that "the fear of the Lord" is the foundation of the Christian faith. As is so frequently quoted, "The fear of the LORD is the *beginning* of wisdom" (Ps. 111:10a). Perhaps the principal reason fathers are failing in the church and throughout the culture and country is that they have largely abandoned the *fear of the Lord*.

The stabilizing *fear of the Lord* has been replaced by fickle feelings and a false love. Consider well and with soberness the dramatic cultural shift of the past two generations. Throughout American history, from our earliest days until the 1960s, a man who could be trusted, whose word was his bond and whose character was deemed "Christian," was commonly referred to as "a God-fearing man." That descriptive phrase has long since left the lips of citizens, both Christian and otherwise, in hot pursuit of self-indulgent "liberty," and often in the very name of Christ. Such a drift has borne consequences both continuing and catastrophic.

Our only hope is to restore the fear of the Lord in God's house.

When both Christians and the broader culture have cast away true faith, founded on the *fear of the Lord*, in unfettered pursuit of supposed *freedom*, our only hope is to restore the *fear of the Lord* in God's house. This is why God cried out to the leaders of Israel, "If then I be a father, where is mine honour? And if I be a master, where is my fear?" (Mal. 1:6).

THE EVER-ELUSIVE "SECRET"

America's only hope—indeed, the world's only hope—is to recover a *secret* . . . God's secret. This *secret* lies at the very foundation of biblical faith and the recovery of biblical fatherhood.

This *secret* is simple to express yet sobering to live out in our families, yes, even in the *family of God*. Yet from God's viewpoint, recovering this *secret* is without equal in reestablishing the functionality of His fatherhood and genuine godly fatherhood on this failing planet. This *secret* is plainly spoken by our Father but profoundly challenging to His sons. The only question before us is, are we up for the challenge?

And now, for the ever-elusive *secret* . . .

> The *secret* of the LORD is with them who fear Him; and He will show them His covenant. . . .
>
> What man is he that feareth the LORD? Him shall He teach in the way that He shall choose (Ps. 25:14, 12).

Sons and daughters must be taught *the fear of the Lord*, yet such a foundational life understanding can only be captured and transmitted by men who truly comprehend and visibly embrace the gravity of God's heart in this regard. "Wherefore now let the fear of the LORD be upon you; take heed and do it: for there is no iniquity with the LORD [y]our God, nor respect of persons. . . . The fear of the LORD prolongeth days, but the years of the wicked shall be shortened" (2 Chron. 19:7; Prov. 10:27).

THE SECRET OF SURE BLESSING

Blessing follows fear . . . The fear of the lord. Surprisingly, God makes no promise of blessing, success, or prosperity to those who do not truly fear Him. Blessing also follows obedience, since anyone who truly fears the Lord will obey Him. This is the synergy of Scripture, resulting in genuine trust, developing love, and further obedience followed by increased favor.

Sons and daughters must be taught the fear of the Lord.

This *fear of the Lord* is not so much a matter of *word* but of *will*. The Father's blessings flow through relationship. Our wills and ways reveal the true value and virtue of that relationship, either confirming or corrupting our words of alleged relationship. Our Father is not impressed by theological complexity or creedal catechism but by a credible relationship revealed in truth and righteous conduct.

THE BLESSED MAN

"Blessed is the man that feareth the LORD, that delighteth greatly in his commandments," observed the Psalmist (Ps. 112:1). Herein lies the key to all the Father's covenantal blessings.

The Father's blessings are extraordinary indeed, but they are also exclusive. They are not relegated only to the wealthy or to those of prominence or pedigree, neither solely to the poor nor to those lacking cultural stature. These blessings are neither offered to the atheist nor to the polytheist, nor even to the monotheist, but only to those who fear the Lord as disclosed exclusively in His inspired Word, the Bible. To argue with the conditions is to argue with the Creator, thereby becoming immediately disqualified.

What, then, are the Father's conditions? We sing, "Praise God, from whom all blessings flow . . . ," but to whom and on what basis do those blessings flow? And if those blessings flow to individual men and their families, what then of congregations . . . even nations?

When it comes to the Father's proferred blessings, His *secrets* are not really *secret*. Rather, they only seem secret because our minds, hearts and ways are not oriented toward His divine viewpoint. "For my thoughts are not your thoughts, neither are your ways my ways, saith the LORD" (Isa. 55:8).

Just as children in a family do not always share the viewpoints of their parents but buck against them, even to their detriment, even so do we resist and rebel against the God who created us in His image (see Gen. 1:26, 3:24). We demand His love and forgiveness but resist His ways that engender His favor born of loving relationship.

How, then, can we recover this seemingly elusive *secret of the Lord*? Is there a clear pathway? And if so, why does the pathway seem so obscure?

RETURNING HEARTS TO THE FATHER

By now it should be abundantly clear that if the hearts of our children are to be turned to their fathers, our own hearts must be returned to the heart of our Heavenly Father. Here, then, is the Father's own prescription—simple, yet profound—"Return unto me," He urges, "and I will return unto you" (Mal. 3:7). But then we find ourselves each asking the same question that Israel did: "*How* shall I return?" Here's how:

SECRET #1—RECOGNIZE GOD AS GOD

Is God really *God*? How do we recognize Him as *God*? How do we demean Him as Father?

Most of the world believes in God, however they may choose to define Him. Even the devils believe in God and tremble (James 2:19). But should the devil or his demons expect God's blessing because they believe *in* Him? Clearly not. So then what kind of belief brings the Father's blessing?

"Return unto me and I will return unto you." (Mal. 3:7)

God, as our Father, is not impressed with whether or not we believe *in* Him. Rather, His Father heart desires that we truly BELIEVE *Him*. This is the fount of the Father's blessing.

The root of the relationship God yearns for among those created in His image is that we truly trust Him . . . that, beginning with a holy fear of incomparable holy respect and awe, we learn to love Him with a whole heart, fervently taking Him, humbly and joyfully at His every word.

The apostle Paul warned of a very contrary viewpoint toward God, the Father, in these end times. "When they knew God, they glorified Him not *as* God . . . Professing themselves to be wise, they became fools" (Rom. 1:21–22). Do we, do you, truly recognize God as *GOD*? Do we believe *Him*, or do we just believe *in* Him? Don't answer too quickly!

When Jesus says, "If ye forgive not men their trespasses, neither will your heavenly Father forgive your trespasses" (Matt. 6:14–15), what do you say? When He says, "Not every one that saith unto me, Lord, Lord, shall enter the kingdom of heaven; but he that doeth the will of my Father which is in heaven" (Matt. 7:21), do you agree, without exception? When Jesus declares, "I am the way, the truth, and the life: no man cometh unto the Father but by me" (John 14:6), what is your response?

When the Father says, "I hate divorce (Mal. 2:16 AMPC), what do you say? When Jesus says, "Whoever shall put away his wife, and marry another, committeth adultery against her" (Mark 10:11), what do you say?

Agreement with the Father is like a symphony. Rather than our wills clashing in cacophony, they sound together in peace and harmony. Blessing follows the pattern of God-fearing ways... that He is God, and we are not.

Agreement with the Father is like a symphony.

Yet we are so prone to reimagine or redefine God according to our own desires, which perverts, distorts and redirects destiny. When we do not agree with God as He reveals himself in Scripture, we actually set ourselves up as competing or surrogate "gods." And God the Father will brook no competition. Blessing is banned, and we are left to our own devices to create our own destiny, however destructive it may be.

This form of exaltation of man's thinking over God's disclosure of Himself has profoundly invaded our churches, our pulpits, our politics and our personal lives. Within this last generation, professing "Christian" women have actually held "Re-imaging God" conferences, fashioning God as a woman. The 1970s spawned the "God is love" movement in the church, which, in exclusive emphasis of love and mercy, reinforced the "free love" movement in the culture, abandoning the biblically based God of truth and judgment in favor of a more "seeker-friendly" face for God. That same generation has witnessed not blessing but a curse coming upon the family, which is the foundation of earthly blessing.

Even the Bible itself has been repeatedly retranslated in order to re-define God in conformity to the evolving mandates of popular culture and "political correctness." When a liberal, secular newsmagazine finally brings focus to our idolatrous re-creating of a culturally preferred "God," speaking like a prophet into the void of spiritual perception and God-fearing preaching in our pulpits, we must know of a certainty that we have forsaken the font of our blessing . . . our Father.

It was time for *Time* to speak. On April 5, 1993, the words emblazoned on the cover of the national newsmagazine declared boldly . . ."THE GENERATION THAT FORGOT GOD." The feature article, titled "The Church Search," made plain the problem. Americans were flooding back to church after the first Persian Gulf War. "But church would never again be the same." Why? What happened? *Time* pierced to the heart of America's religious rebellion, declaring, "Americans are looking for a custom-made god, one made in their own image."

If necessary, God can publish His warnings even through pagan writings when His pastors and prophets are silent. *Time* concluded its lengthy feature article with a baneful lament.

> Wouldn't it be sad that after flooding back to church, rather than the glorification of God we achieved only the gratification of man?[1]

We must return to recognizing God as *God* . . . not the "god" we wish Him to be, but the God that He is. It is our only hope for genuine happiness, which comes only from the God from whom all blessings flow . . . the Father.

SECRET #2—DELIGHT IN GOD'S WORD

The real issue is authority . . . the Father's authority in His household. When we recognize God as *God*, we are then in a place where we can legitimately experience *the fear of the Lord*. The true fear of the Lord, the key to God's "secret," brings us within the ambit or realm of His authority so that our ways can be blessed. His ways then become our ways, His wisdom becomes our wisdom, and His Word becomes our word.

For this reason the Psalmist wrote, "Blessed is the man that feareth the Lord, that delighteth greatly in his commandments" (Ps. 112:1). It is not enough to tacitly recognize the Scriptures cognitively as the Word of God. They must be embraced in their fullness. We must "delight" in them . . . all of them. Our delight must not be some abstract concept but must be revealed in absolute conviction of heart and mind. It is a daily endeavor.

The blessed man's "delight is in the law of the Lord: and in His law doth he meditate day and night" (Ps. 1:2). Remember: "The secret of the Lord is with them that fear him: and he will shew them his covenant" (Ps. 25:14). When God, the "I AM" (Exod. 3:14–15), reveals His covenant, and we walk in it, blessing will become both our heritage and our legacy. "Blessed are they that keep his testimonies, and that seek him with a whole heart. . . . Then shall I not be ashamed, when I have respect unto *all* thy commandments" (Ps. 119:2, 6).

"The secret of the Lord is with them that fear him." (Ps. 25:14).

"What man is he that feareth the LORD? him shall he teach in the way that he shall choose" (Ps. 25:12). "Thy words were found, and I did eat them; and thy word was unto me the joy and rejoicing of mine heart" (Jer. 15:16).

SECRET #3—OBEY GOD'S WORD AND WILL

"The fear of the LORD is the instruction of wisdom; and before honour is humility" (Prov. 15:33). To be blessed of God is to be honored by Him. Yet to be honored by God, we must be submitted to His lordship in humility as true sons.

When we truly walk in the genuine fear of the Lord, it brings us to a place of humility, recognizing that He truly is God. When we, from the heart, recognize that He really is *God*, His Word and will become of preeminent import in our lives, leading us to obey . . . to be "doers of the word, and not hearers only, deceiving [our] own selves" (James 1:22). Blessing follows.

Recognizing that God is actually *God* exalts His authority in our lives. As we submit willingly and joyfully to our Father's authority in the household of faith, we become the beneficiaries of His blessings. We begin to trust Him. Love develops. We obey as an increasing expression of our increasing trust. Faith and love emerge as the prominent heart motivations to obedience. Favor increases. The relationship our natural minds once spurned now becomes a righteous and delightsome reality.

SECRET #4—PRAISE GOD AS GOD

Most people would rather praise than pray. We are all prone to pray and praise rather than obey. Why is that pattern so prevalent in our spiritual practice? It is because of our perpetual struggle in truly seeing and embracing God as *God*.

Before He is our *Father*, He is GOD.

We somehow resist obedience as defiling our desire for relationship and as a condition for His blessing. We claim God's supposed "unconditional love" and grace while spurning His unconditional requirement that we truly see, treat and relate to Him as "God" rather than as a cuddly teddy bear or as a cosmic Santa Claus.

Our praise, therefore, must be preceded by a genuine fear of the Lord if it is to be genuine praise. The word *praise* and its various forms appears at least 179 times in the Psalms, most of which are ascribed to David, whom God described as "a man after mine own heart" (Acts 13:22). If we are to praise God as a man "after God's own heart," it is prerequisite that we deeply honor and respect His genuine Godhood.

"God and God alone/ is fit to take the universe's throne," sings gospel artist Steve Green. "Let everything that lives/ reserve its truest praise/ for God and God alone."[2] The Psalmist repeatedly echoed the theme:

> Praise ye the LORD. *Blessed is the man that feareth the LORD, that delighteth greatly in his commandments.* (Ps. 112:1)

> Praise ye the LORD. . . . Blessed are they that keep judgment and that doeth righteousness at all time. (Ps. 106:1, 3)

> The LORD is great and greatly to be praised: *he is to be feared* above all gods. (Ps. 96:4)

> *The Lord reigneth; let the people tremble.* . . . Let them praise thy great and terrible name; for it is holy. . . . Exalt ye the LORD our God, and worship at his footstool; for he is holy. (Ps. 99:1–5)

Teach me thy way, O LORD; I will walk in thy truth: *unite my heart to fear thy name*. I will praise thee, O Lord my God, with all my heart: and I will glorify thy name for evermore. (Ps. 86:11–12)

I will praise thee with my whole heart. . . . I will worship . . . and praise thy name for thy lovingkindness and for thy truth: for thou hast magnified thy word above all thy name. (Ps. 138:1–2)

Genuine praise, recognizing God as *God*, delighting in His Word, while humbly obeying His Word and will are the underlying "secrets" to God's blessing. Notice! God has magnified or exalted His Word even above His own name (Ps. 138:2). We cannot rightly claim His name or the blessings that flow from His holy promises if we fail to embrace fully and follow the fullness of His revealed Word. To do so is an illegitimate and fraudulent effort to gain by spiritual subterfuge that which is not rightly ours, bringing a curse rather than a blessing.

The gravity of this egregious effort to claim Father's blessings while spurning His authority as God is dramatically detailed in Paul's epistle to the church at Rome. It stands against and reveals the heart of our perpetual pursuit of redefining, redesigning and even repudiating what God has said in His Word in order to serve the false gods of cultural mandates and majorities, religious pluralism, multiculturalism and political "correctness." Consider well the warning:

For the wrath of God is revealed from heaven against all ungodliness and unrighteousness of men, who hold the truth in unrighteousness. . . . because that when they knew God, *they glorified him not as God,* neither were thankful; but became vain in their imagination, and their foolish heart was darkened. Professing themselves to be wise, they became fools . . . Wherefore God gave them up to uncleanness through the lusts of their own hearts . . . who changed the truth of God into a lie, and worshipped and served the creature more than the Creator . . . For this cause God gave them up unto vile affections. . . . And even as they did not like to retain God [as *God*] in their knowledge, God gave them up to a reprobate mind to do those things that are not convenient [not righteous before God]. . . . who knowing the judgment of God, that they which commit such things are worthy of death, not only do the same, but have pleasure in [approve] them that do them. (Rom. 1:18–32)

OUR HOPE IN TRUE HONOR

Genuine blessing follows the genuine *fear of the Lord.* To place . . . or replace . . . ourselves in the place of God's blessing, we must restore the *fear of the Lord.* The chief factor to which we can attribute the waning blessings of God in the United States of America is the wanton disregard—indeed, disdain—of the fear of the Lord, from the church house to the White House and from pulpit to pew, so that even our praise has become perverted.

Genuine blessing follows the genuine fear of the Lord.

Since the mid-1960s, the American people and their pastors, politicians, professors and presidents have run furiously from the fear of the Lord in every sphere from church to culture. The sociological and financial statistics of this generation reveal the banning of God's blessing and the withdrawal of His holy favor.

Regardless of where we look, we see the clear signs of divine abandonment of a nation that once was internationally known as walking in the fear of the Lord. Her praise is now preempted by her promiscuity and profligacy while her politicians struggle with bankruptcy. Her parents promise protection while abandoning their promise to God and to their progeny through treachery, forsaking vows in reckless abandonment of the fear of the Lord (Mal. 2:13–17).

It is said that "hope springs eternal in the human heart." Yet the hope of America . . . indeed, the entire Western world . . . is rapidly turning to a hellish horror in the wake of false worship and daring abandonment of the fear of the Lord.

Our only hope, our only light for a future anyone would truly care to experience, is to restore the fear of the Lord in our lives, one person at a time, beginning with you and me. It will not begin with "the other guy." Restoring true honor of the Father will renew hope for the future.

Time is short! Jesus, the Messiah, is coming soon. Today, if you will hear His voice, harden not your heart. "Surely His salvation is nigh them that fear him; that glory may dwell in our land" (Ps. 85:9).

PROBING OUR HEARTS

1. In what ways has our radical abandonment of the *fear of the Lord*, both in the culture and in the church, resulted in failure of fatherhood?

   NOTE: This may be the most probing and serious question to be answered by both physical and spiritual fathers.

2. Do you agree, or disagree, that America's only hope . . . even the world's only hope . . . is to recover God's secret—the link between the *fear of the Lord* and the blessings of His covenant? Why . . . or why not?

3. What do you think the Father was thinking when He inspired use of the phrase *the fear of the Lord*? Why, in our generation, are we so prone to shrink from and even revise that phrase in some *modern* Bible translations?

4. *Time* magazine, in 1993, declared America "The GENERATION THAT FORGOT GOD," and went on to say that Americans were, even at that time, "looking for a custom-made god, one made in their own image." Can you see from that observation that we had then and have long since abandoned God as *GOD*, thus rejecting the fear of the Lord?

5. In what way is the fear of the Lord the foundation of both wisdom and our willingness to submit to Father's authority?

6. What can we conclude from the Psalmist's words "Surely His salvation is nigh them that fear him; that glory may dwell in our land"?

10

FAITH *IN* THE FATHER

A mark of maturity, or immaturity, in a man is the way he functions as a father in his home.

—GENE A. GETZ

A FATHER'S GREATEST DESIRE is that he be respected by his wife and be trusted by his children. Each of these desires is facing near catastrophic destruction from the assault of a post-modern, God-despising culture in hot pursuit of SELF. Since "the time is come that judgment must begin at the house of God" (1 Peter 4:17), how should we, as men and fathers, then live?

DECISION FOLLOWS DESIRE
Most men *desire*, but few decide. Even fewer follow decision with diligence that changes destiny.

Interestingly, our relationship with God as men is manifested through two metaphors throughout the Bible.

First, we are described as the "bride" of Christ (see Mark 2:19–20).

Second, we are described as "the children of God" as Father (Rom. 8:16; Gal. 3:26).

Most men desire, but few decide.

When we, as men and as earthly husbands and fathers, fail to truly respect and honor Jesus Christ as the Bridegroom, we necessarily lose the respect and honor we so crave from our wives. Similarly, when we fail to trust and obey our heavenly Father, we lose the necessary and longed-for trust and obedience of our own sons and daughters. These interconnections are divinely interwoven in the Creator's design for His family, our families, and for the future of all created in His image. It should, then, come as no surprise that these interconnections and interdependencies are under such persistent attack by the archenemy of our very souls.

Our response to this destructive dilemma on the cusp of Christ's second coming will require us to not only *desire* but *decide* to truly restore our faith in our Father. And that decision must then be effectuated by *diligence* if we would change *destiny*. Whether or not we leave a legacy that lasts will depend on at least seven essential trues that will bring us to triumph in the end. The only condition is that we "through faith and patience inherit the promises" (Heb. 6:12).

SEVEN TRIUMPHANT TRUES

All of the Father's principles, or *trues*, are taught and transmitted "precept upon precept; line upon line" (Isa. 28:10). If we earthly fathers are to truly leave a legacy that lasts, we must grasp the long-term, enduring simplicity of this foundational precept if we are to experience a fulfilling, yes, even triumphant end to our fathering labors. There will not be, nor can be, any effort to make an "end run" around this sevenfold progression. And time will tell the tale through many trials and testings.

TURNING. If we, as fathers, desire and expect our children to turn toward us, we must first turn back toward the Father.

Turning and returning are our Father's absolute prerequisites to the fulfillment of His plan and promises in and for our lives as fathers. Yet in order for us to engage with the Father in His family enterprise, we must first recognize as "children" that we have, either in whole or in part, strayed from His ways and therefore frustrated His fellowship.

Expect our children to turn toward us, we must first turn back toward the Father.

Turning and returning are the fulcrum of restored and righteous fellowship with the Father. As cried the Psalmist, "Turn us again, O God, and cause thy face to shine; and we shall be saved. O LORD God of hosts, how long wilt thou be angry against the prayer of thy people?" And again, "Turn us, O God of our salvation; and cause thine anger toward us to cease" (Ps. 80:3–4; 85:4).

Seek ye the LORD [Father] while he may be found . . .

Let the wicked [or wayward son] forsake his way, and the unrighteous man his thoughts: and *let him return* unto the Lord, and he will have mercy upon him; and to our God [Father], for he will abundantly pardon.

For my [Fatherly] thoughts are not your thoughts, neither are your ways my [Fatherly] ways, saith the LORD. (Isa. 55:6–8)

"I am a father to Israel," saith the Lord, and Israel has bemoaned saying, "Thou hast chastised me." Yet I, as Israel, now cry to you as my Father, "Turn thou me, and I shall be turned; for thou art the LORD my God" (Jer. 31:9, 18). The Father is patiently awaiting this plaintiff cry from those who profess to be His sons.

TRUST. In turning and returning, *trust* can now be in the process of restoration; first with the Father, then with our own sons and daughters.

Turning precedes trust, and trust precedes our ability to effectively teach or receive truth. The holiness of truth is otherwise colored or camouflaged by hypocrisy, which harms our yearned-for legacy.

Trust is established first in "the fear of the Lord," resulting progressively in faith *in* the Lord our Father. Faith is progressively revealed in obedience *to* the Father, inuring through time to increasing trust.

Therefore, as fathers, we are urged . . . even commanded . . . to:

Trust in the LORD [our Father] with all thine heart: and lean not unto thine own understanding. In all thy ways acknowledge him and he shall direct thy paths. Be not wise in thine own eyes: fear the LORD and depart from evil. . . . Whoso trusteth in the Lord, happy is he. (Prov. 3:5–7; 16:20)

TRUTH. The very concept of *truth* is rapidly becoming obsolete throughout Western culture. Fewer than 50 percent of professing Christians now believe in absolute truth, and less than 10 percent of our younger generation claiming the name of Christ admit to anything approaching absolute truth. Shockingly, only 20 percent of those professing Christians under thirty-five believe that Jesus Christ is the only Savior, "the way, the truth, and the life," and that "no one comes to the Father" but through Him (John 14:6 NKJV).

This should indeed be frightening for concerned fathers. Why? Because the wrath of God the Father continues to rest on our falsely led sons and daughters who are not convinced through personal conviction to conversion of heart that only "He that believeth on the Son hath everlasting life" and that "he that believeth not on the Son [as the sole means of salvation] shall not see life; but the wrath of God abideth on him" (John 3:36).

You ask, then, "Wherein lies the problem? How could we, in a purportedly 'Christian' country with such an amazing godly heritage, have reached such a horrific state of affairs?" Aside from the daring and progressive abandonment of the fear of the Lord throughout the culture, the troubling truth is that "Christian" fathers have also progressively abandoned the living truth of the Word of the Father in hot pursuit of cultural prosperity. Principled, faith-filled living has been painfully sacrificed on the altar of pragmatism.

In effect, professing Christian fathers have fostered an "Esau" generation, willing to sacrifice the promises of the eternal verities of the Father's Word and Ways in pursuit of the short-term perceived promises of personal peace and prosperity (Gen. 25:30–34). The accumulated pain of such *Esau* thinking is palpable and easily perceived throughout not only the culture but also the church.

How then can we recover and restore "the years that the locusts hath eaten" (Joel 2:25)? We must restore our love of truth—the Father's truth—and make it visibly and vibrantly active throughout our households, beginning in our own life ways. And we have a model to follow.

Jesus made it clear as the only begotten Son of the Father. "I do nothing of myself; but as my Father hath taught me, I speak these things . . . I do always the things that please him." And then the Son declared, "If ye continue in my word, then are ye my disciples indeed; and ye shall know the *truth* and the *truth* shall make you free" (John 8:28–32).

If trust is our hope for our sons and daughters, truth must become a passionate pursuit by fathers who display their love of the truth as a visible happening in the household.

TEACHING. Truth is the foundation for all legitimate teaching that hopes to yield a godly legacy. Unfortunately, since truth has fallen on hard times in our day, the *teaching* of truth has likewise waned and our legacies are in jeopardy.

Lamentably, we are now known for "ever learning" but seldom coming to "the knowledge of the truth." The tendency, instead, is to "resist the truth," leaving us with increasingly corrupt minds, "reprobate concerning the faith." Indeed, and in truth, these are the prophesied "perilous times" of which Paul wrote (2 Tim. 3:7, 8, 1). And our sons and daughters are therefore in peril.

How can this perilous and terrifying trajectory be changed? Truly we, as fathers and grandfathers, must reembrace our essential role as teachers, both by precept and example. And in order to fulfill that responsibility responsibly, we must again be lovers of truth.

The apostle Paul aptly described our dilemma. It is the dilemma of our day, and destiny rides in the balance. Deception and destruction are even now knocking at our doors.

The "deceivableness of unrighteousness" is given sway in our homes and even ministries "because [we] receive not the love of the truth." And because of this lack of passionate love of the truth, we are prevented from carrying a persistent teaching to those we love that would protect them from "strong delusion" and the "lie" that is invading our families, destroying the very foundations of our faith and future. Will our progeny, then, be trapped in the devices of the Destroyer and be "damned" because they "believed not the truth" but had "pleasure in unrighteousness" (2 Thess. 2:9–12)?

When only 20 percent of professing Christians of the Millennial generation believe that Jesus Christ is the only way, the only truth and the only life—the only way to the Father—the gravity of the moment for our generation is beyond desperate.

It is past time for teachers of truth to be resurrected from the collective rubble in which our children and grandchildren wallow. Yet as the apostle Paul lamented, "Where for a time ye ought to be teachers, ye have need that one teach you again which be the first principles of the oracles of God; and are become such as have need of milk, and not of strong meat. For every one that useth milk is unskillful in the word of unrighteousness: for he is a babe" (Heb. 5:12–13).

What, then, shall we do? The times are in our hands. The Father has deputized all fathers and grandfathers and spiritual fathers for such a time as this. We dare not opt out of this holy calling. As it is written . . .

> These words, which I command thee this day, shall be in thine heart: And thou shalt *teach them diligently* unto thy children and shalt talk of them . . . When thou sittest in thine house; When thou walkest by the way; When thou liest down; and When thou risest up. (Deut. 6:6–7)

TRAINING. "Train up a child in the way he should go," we are told, and the likelihood is much greater that "when he is old he shall not depart from it" (Prov. 22:6).

Teaching is essential but must be followed by *training*. Although teaching requires a father's time, training demands greater dedication of time and personal attention so that the precepts taught are properly and consistently applied in the child's actions and attitudes.

Genuine and consistent application of spiritual truth is almost invariably the missing link in most "teaching" of the Father's Word. For that reason, the truth is rejected as irrelevant, and transformation seldom takes place. This is the plight of both pastor and parishioner. Paralyzed by fear of rejection, those charged with fatherly teaching and training are reluctant to make the applications of the Father's truth that are most likely to produce profound change. The risk of personal rejection is deemed too great. In reality, we are just not ready to "go to the cross" with Jesus, who lovingly, yet boldly, took those risks with a long-range view to eternal destiny.

Here is a fundamental and guiding principle declared often on *Viewpoint*, our national radio program "confronting the deepest issues of America's heart and home from God's eternal perspective."

> Information without transformation yields frustration, stagnation, and often termination. Application is the only bridge from information to transformation.

Our Father is watching over His Word to perform it. But we, as deputized fathers, must present that Word in such a way that the Holy Spirit can truly transform our sons and daughters—yes, pastors and our parishioners too—through conviction of heart and conversion of mind. The Father is longing for a few good men who, as lovers of His truth, will both *teach* and *train* the generation that may well see the Second Coming.

TESTING. Trust will inevitably be tested. In fact, trust must and will be tested to be periodically validated.

The legacy we leave will largely be measured by how our children perceive we pass the test of their trust. And that perception is formed not by a single event but by simple consistency of trustworthiness. As children find they can trust their father's promises and practices, so the foundation is laid, line upon line, for their ability to trust the heavenly Father with joyful yet patient expectation.

The legacy we leave will largely be measured by how our children perceive we pass the test of their trust.

The trust of Jesus was immediately and purposefully tested upon His baptism. He was "led up of the Spirit into the wilderness to be tempted [tested] of the devil" (Matt. 4:1). Three times, in three serious ways, the trust of the Messiah, as a Son, was severely tested. The question loomed large for all history. Was the Father's Word and will to be trusted? The legacy of humankind lay in the balance.

Even so, in ways that determine the legacy we leave as fathers, we are similarly tested and tried? The measure of the legacy we leave will be largely defined by our pattern of passing the test of trustworthiness with our sons and daughters.

Yet, in a more profound and even troubling sense, the legacy of trust we leave with our progeny will be determined by their perception of whether or not we pass the test of persistent trust in the Father. Just as Jesus was tested as a Son, so we are tested as sons to determine the truth of our alleged trust. And just as the then and future followers of our Lord (children of the Father) would be secured by the victorious truth of the Savior, so will our own sons and daughters be more likely to be saved because of our persistent trust that they can observe through the obvious tests that come our way.

TRIBULATION. Severe testing builds substantial trust. Trust is built and strengthened through its exercise. It is called *faith*.

And without such increasing faith built of tested trust, "it is impossible to please [the Father]: for he that cometh to God [the Father] must believe [not only] that he is, but that he is a rewarder of them that diligently seek him" (Heb. 11:6).

Tribulation of fathers becomes essential for their sons to pass the trust test, both of their fathers and of the Father. Our *attitudes* toward tribulation will often determine the *actions* of our children, both toward us and toward God. Legacy therefore brings pending severe testing that reveals either genuine or counterfeit trust.

Jesus made it abundantly clear. "In the world ye shall have tribulation: but be of good cheer, I have overcome the world" (John 16:33). In a diminished sense, we also, having victoriously endured tribulation, can encourage our own children, saying, "Be of good courage. I have been seriously tested and have overcome, and so can you."

Legacy brings severe testing that reveals either genuine or counterfeit trust.

The Son of the Father admonished us in advance as to the walk we fathers should anticipate in order to raise up God-fearing and God-following children. He did not promise us an easy road defined by three easy steps to success. Rather, He inspired us through successful testing that we, like He, can leave a legacy that will last for eternity.

James, the brother of our Lord, well understood the significance of this pattern of testing, trials, and tribulation. He admonished us:

My brethren, count it all joy when ye fall into divers [many] temptations [trials and tribulations]; knowing this, that the trying of your faith worketh patience. But let patience have her perfect work, that you might be perfect and entire, wanting nothing. (James 1:2–4)

The theme is consistent throughout both Old and New Testaments. Faith and trust must be tested, often severely, if we are to be proven as true sons. Consider, and let these faith-building declarations strengthen our fatherly hearts in these trying times.

"We glory in tribulations." (Rom. 5:3)

"[Be] patient in tribulation." (Rom. 12:12)

"I am exceeding joyful in tribulation." (2 Cor. 7:4)

"We should suffer tribulation." (1 Thess. 3:4)

"Faint not at my tribulations." (Eph. 3:13)

"We must through much tribulation enter into the kingdom of God." (Acts 14:22)

TRIUMPH. Testing and tribulation always precede *triumph*. If there is no battle, no struggle, there is no possible victory. Victory always follows successful testing through some measure of tribulation.

The Father is, even now, seeking true fathers who will prepare their sons and daughters for coming times of greater testing of trust and faith. But that will not happen unless the hearts of the fathers are truly turned toward their children and the children, in turn, are seeking their fathers' proven faith. Eternal destiny, for many, is at stake.

Testing and tribulation always precede triumph.

The Father's heart is in hot pursuit of the hearts of fathers for such a time as this. Just as the Son advised His spiritual sons, the apostles, "It is not for you to know the times or the seasons which the Father hath put in his own power" (Acts 1:7), even so we may not absolutely know and recognize the severity of the hour, but the Father does. And as a good and righteous Father, He is wooing and warning all fathers to prepare the way of the Lord, lest the deceiver's final deceptive assault sweep away both us and our children to perdition.

This is the *Elijah* moment. History hinges on our decisions as dads. Procrastination is not possible if we would prevail victoriously. Legacy lurks in the spiritual liability flowing from the testing that is now at the door.

> Beloved now are we the sons of God . . . and every man that hath this hope in him purifieth himself, even as he is pure. (1 John 3:2–3)

Let us, like the firstborn Son, Jesus, be about the Father's business (Luke 2:44), for time is knocking at the door of eternity even now.

PROBING OUR HEARTS

1. If we fathers would change destiny, we must embrace godly desire, confirmed by heart decision and effectuated by diligence. At which of these points do you find yourself either flailing or failing? Why? How will you change?

2. As you read about the "Seven Triumphant Trues," did you find any of these to be a point of stumbling in your life as one who seeks to be a godly father? Why do you think you have stumbled in that area? Are you prepared to change?

3. If your wife were to rate your success and faithfulness in practicing the Seven Triumphant Trues, as a whole, where do you honestly believe she would rate you on a scale of 1 to 10, with 10 being the most faithful?

4. Where do you think the Father would rate you on the same scale?

5. If you were totally convinced in both mind and heart that if you would make the necessary choices, the Father would assist you by His Spirit in making the necessary changes, would it, in reality, make any real difference in your life pattern?

11

FROM PATER TO PATRIARCH

As a priest you represent your family to God; as a prophet you represent God to your family.

—DEREK PRINCE

THE FATHER OF FATHERS is looking for a man among men. He is searching for a few good and godly men who stand strong and stalwart in a generation that is increasingly swayed by the winds of worldly change. Such men are rare. They have moved far beyond boyhood to manhood, yet see a greater calling— the need to be a man among men, a father among fathers—a man whose life to which our sons and daughters can aspire and who, by God's grace, can inspire the next generation and generations to come.

PATER OR PATRIARCH

Will I be a mere *pater,* or mature to become a *patriarch*? This is the choice and challenge of every man, and our decision will determine the destiny of many as well as our legacy.

The word *patriarch* (or *patriarchs*) occurs only four times in the King James Version, and interestingly, all four times in the New Testament—three times in the book of Acts and once in the book of Hebrews. These appearances are particularly poignant since, of all the New Testament books, Acts and Hebrews most particularly point to those in the past who set the spiritual course for the future.

By contrast, the word *father* and its various forms appears literally hundreds of times throughout Scripture—too many to merit an actual count. Obviously, the word *father* is of critical and oft-repeatable significance to the Father. When a father persistently repeats himself, the children should take heed and seek to discern the *why* behind the repetition.

It is patriarchy that produces a powerful legacy that lasts.

Perhaps one might conclude, then, that the far lesser use or appearance of the word *patriarch* might indicate a lesser significance than the word *father*. On the other hand, that which stands out uniquely among the many may actually carry the greater weight, impact . . . indeed, legacy potential . . . precisely because it manifests a higher or more potent dimension of fatherhood. It would seem, then, that this higher standard of fathering is the standard toward which we must strive by grace through faith.

The Latin word for "father" is *pater*. Pater-hood is worthy and desperately needed. Patriarchy, by contrast, is the consummate role to be realized by every father. It is patriarchy that produces a powerful legacy that lasts, that endures the tests of turbulent waters threatening generations.

CONTRASTS THAT COUNT

From time to time a deep yearning wells up within the masculine mind and heart—a yearning for significance beyond the simple and seemingly repetitive tasks that commonly define us as men. That yearning may emerge with varying degrees of intensity depending on our personal history and the season of our life. But it is nevertheless there, knocking for recognition amid the business or boring sameness that continually hovers over performance of our daily duties.

That internal nudge is the Father's investment of a normal progression of manhood and fatherhood characteristic of and deeply rooted in His own divine expression of Fatherhood. Rather than give us "a piece of His mind," He seeks to promote in us a deep yearning from His own Fatherly heart. It is an intangible desire to become more than a mere man, to foster and be fulfilled by something beyond being a faithful father. It is the unspoken, yet deeply felt calling, to become a patriarch—a calling that few acknowledge hearing and even fewer heed.

To understand the mind and heart of a patriarch, perhaps the most understandable way is to paint a few contrasts. These contrasts are critical in our ability to perceive or discern the differences in the stages of a man's development toward spiritual maturity. Any attempt to discount these differences will eventually frustrate our ultimate fulfillment in pursuit of godly fathering.

FROM BOYHOOD TO MANHOOD

We began at boyhood, the gateway to manhood. "Boys will be boys," we often say. And as a general expression, it is an aphorism that is persuasive because it is pervasively true. Why is it true? Because boys think and behave like boys. Their concern is lacking any real sense of consequence. Boys, in their immaturity, generally do not consider others. Their focus and driving force is the ever-present ME. Others are relatively insignificant unless seen as the source of "what I want." That is the defining description of a generation now commonly known as *Millennials*.

While at a time Millennials should be entering manhood, they remain largely limited in thought and behavior to boyhood. While broadly aged from eighteen to thirty-five, they seem addicted to boyhood realities and expectations demonstrated publicly and privately as entitlement and irresponsibility. This failure to emerge from boyhood to manhood has become a plague morally, spiritually and financially upon the current generation, which depended upon their natural progression to maturity. This destructive dilemma has been aptly described as "failure to launch."

We wonder how such a shocking disconnect might have occurred. How might an entire generation have become so paralyzed in the perpetual pursuit of self?

The answer is not difficult to identify, but is exceedingly painful to admit. It is deeply rooted in their fathers, and even grandfathers, who failed to successfully advance from boyhood to manhood and fatherhood, thus sowing the early seeds of entitlement and irresponsibility. True fathers have been few, and patriarchs almost passé. What the fathers and grandfathers have portrayed in moderation, their progeny have displayed in excess.

Thus, perpetual boyhood largely defines the upcoming generation of cultural leaders, defining a future of ever-diminished fatherhood.

FROM MANHOOD TO FATHERHOOD

Throughout history, in virtually every culture, as boys emerged into manhood, they were expected to take on the social and cultural characteristics of a *man*. Such cultural expectation not only drew the boy further into manhood, but propelled him by an inward desire to truly become a man, taking on manly privileges and responsibilities. These natural and historical forces have now become so diminished as to threaten the demise of genuine manhood.

From the late 1960s to the present, the force of the feminist movement has significantly defined and driven this decline. Men have been systematically demasculinized. And lamentably, the pervasive force of this movement has permeated the church and her ministry, gradually undermining the male role in spiritual leadership and the family. Genuine fatherhood then became the progressive casualty of deteriorated manhood.

FROM FATHERHOOD TO PATRIARCHY

The incessant cry of the feminist revolution was and is the destruction of this allegedly "evil" patriarchal society. For the past two generations, the cultural war against manhood and fatherhood has dramatically altered the biblical balance of the role of men and women as ordained by God, the Father. The engine of political correctness has served to define this deviancy ever downward into a culturally demanded feminine "mystique," overpowering both manhood and ministry.

Fathers have been decidedly diminished and fatherhood derided. The church, through its mainline expressions, led the way in embracing the secularly redefined norms. The evangelical churches adopted their own version of the feminist values, replacing facts and genuine faith with feelings. Individual feelings have replaced the Holy Spirit, and God the Father is irreverently demeaned as irrelevant . . . just a mean-spirited and dogmatic Old Testament God relegated to the distant past who just doesn't quite understand our new and revised "gospel" message of good feelings and elevated self-esteem.

Fathers now face an epic battle and fatherhood is under massive assault. The media perpetually characterizes men, and particularly fathers, as insignificant, bumbling boys while our churches, perhaps somewhat unwittingly, demasculinize ministry. Men and fathers now struggle for meaningful identity, leaving our children largely estranged from an environment of genuine fatherhood. The *metrosexual* model has redefined as *desirable* men as androgynous creatures, sanitized of a masculine mind, transforming the yearning for biblical patriarchy into a cultural prison as virtual eunuchs.

Fathers now face an epic battle.

This persistent pressure over at least two generations has nearly destroyed the foundations of a true patriarch among the people . . . a generation that might well see the Second Coming of Christ. It is little wonder, then, that the Father should passionately desire to call the hearts of the fathers to the children and the hearts of the children to the fathers in this momentous hour of history. But what of the *patriarch*? Is this a foreign concept, or is it one with which we should be familiar? And if the foundations be largely destroyed, what can, and should, the righteous do?

PROPHECY AND THE PATRIARCH

Where there is a patriarch, there is a prophetic implication, if not prophesy, for the future. The biblical patriarchs were an implicit, if not explicit, part of the Father's prophetic plan for His people—His greater family.

While the patriarchs of Israel's past were by no means perfect, they nevertheless bore the mantle of the Father's mission for those who would follow in the path they paved. Their faith, however inadequately expressed, defined the future destiny of the family of the Father, and echos beyond their time to our time. Therefore, patriarchs are of profound significance in the divine plan and purpose of history, which is HIS STORY in the earth.

Vision, coupled with a deep sense of calling, is the defining character of a true patriarch. Yet every "patriarch" begins his journey as a boy, progressing in defined order to manhood and fatherhood, out of which emerges the destiny-defining role of a patriarch. What, then, differentiates a father from a patriarch?

The heart, opened to a greater hope than the relative vanities of manhood and fatherhood, begins to define a path and broader purpose beyond the mere care of limited personal affairs to a largeness of destiny-defining influence. Such influence cannot be created by selfishly driven aspiration or by pride-driven ambition, but is developed by persistent, faithful obedience to the Father's plan and purposes in continual view of the Father's promises. When this pattern of life becomes deeply ingrained in the will and ways of a father—even in the ways of a childless man—the spirit of a patriarch begins to emerge and becomes recognizable.

While fatherhood is itself fulfilling, it bears little resemblance to the overwhelming inner joy and fulfillment of a patriarch. However, to whom much is given, much more is required. For this reason, the burden borne by the emerging patriarch is commensurate to the increasing blessing. This is the path of godly maturity the Father desires for men who would be fathers. It is not the Father alone who waits for us to win in this eternal battle of the flesh, but our children and grandchildren.

Will you be a pater or a patriarch?

When will the hearts of the fathers be truly turned toward their children, and the hearts of the children be truly turned toward their fathers? Time will determine the trajectory of history, but that "time" is in our time—yours and mine.

Will I, will you, be a *pater* . . . or a *patriarch*?

PROBING OUR HEARTS

1. What characteristics (other than physical) distinguish a *boy* from a *man*?

2. How might you distinguish (other than by age) the average *man* or father from a *patriarch*?

3. Why do you think the patriarchs of the Bible are seen in both New and Old Testaments as setting the spiritual course for the future?

4. What changes in thought, attitude, behavior and priorities would be needed for you to move from being a faithful father to becoming a patriarch?

5. Do you desire to become, as it were, a patriarch in your generation? Why . . . or why not?

12

THE FOLLY OF FATHERLESSNESS

Ninety-three percent of all people in prison are male, and 85 percent of them have no father figure.

—PATRICK MORLEY

FATHERLESSNESS IS A CURSE. From the Father's viewpoint, the absence of or abandonment by fathers is a consummate curse. It is an ultimate and consuming curse on creation.

WHY HAVE YOU FORSAKEN ME?

When Christ cried out from the cross, "My God, My God, why hast thou forsaken me?" (Matt. 27:46), Jesus experienced this terrifying curse of sin. The sense of absolute abandonment at the moment of crucifixion became the crucible out of which our hope as fathers and fathers-to-be would be restored. As the only begotten and sinless Son experienced the gut-wrenching alienation from the Father, we who would truly embrace His sacrifice would be spared eternal alienation from the Father. Even as Christ bore the agonizing burden of our sin and separation, we can become the agents of eternal and temporal reconciliation, both with the Father, and with our sons and daughters.

Lest we should question the profound passion of perceived Fatherly abandonment Christ suffered, we are reminded that His words immediately before the Father's lifting of Fatherly protection from the Son were, "Father forgive them; for they know not what they do" (Luke 23:34).

Sin separates. Our sin separates and separated us from the Father. The pure obedience of Jesus, as the only begotten Son, enabled Him to take upon Himself through eternal sacrifice the curse of separation, that we might experience, by faith, the adoption as sons, "whereby we cry, Abba, Father" (Rom. 8:15).

With such hope amid the horror of separation, why then has fatherlessness, both physical and spiritual, become a defining characteristic of our time? How could such a thing be if we are truly awaiting the second coming of Christ—the "blessed hope" of the Church (Titus 2:13)? That is a rhetorical question we must all attempt to answer, probing the deepest recesses of our own hearts and homes—as are these:

> In what ways, either large or seemingly small, have my own attitudes and actions contributed to the greater culture of fatherlessness?

> What have I done . . . or not done . . . that likely has portrayed or displayed a false or unfaithful image of both good and godly fatherhood?

If my example were replicated ten million times, what might the effect have been in defining the Father's model of fathering throughout the nation?

Has the Holy Spirit nudged me from time to time on these points? How have I responded?

Have I resisted, procrastinated, given temporary lip service . . . or just ignored Him?

The Father is insisting that our time is NOW. The ultimate moments of history—HIS STORY—are upon us. To delay or dispute is to invite destruction. We must change our *want-to's* to conform to the Father's will. The alternative is a final, cumulative and catastrophic implementation of earth's end-time cultural curse, as Malachi so aptly warned (Mal. 4:5–6). What spiritual and statistical evidence will define and determine our legacy?

The Father is insisting that our time is NOW!

Perhaps a stark picture portrayed by current statistics will help us get a better grip on the horror . . . or hope . . . that lies before us based on the choices we make.

THE FOLLIES OF FATHERLESSNESS

Statistics showing trends in society are the simplest way to depict the dire direction of the culture. They also reflect the consequences of underlying spiritual strength or weakness.

The statistics presented here, in summary, are incontrovertible and almost universally accepted by most social observers, regardless of politics or personal religious persuasion. Arguments are presented and positions taken as to underlying causes, but the consequences, regardless of cause, are clear and progressively catastrophic. Efforts by pastors and politicians to trifle with these truths serve only to declare a steadfast unwillingness both to face the truth and to respond in any meaningful way to the truth that is literally slapping us all in the face.

Strap on your fatherly seatbelt as we take this statistical journey over severely unmaintained roads not normally welcoming to motor vehicles.

We first listen to the travel warnings of those who have devoted their lives to protecting and preserving fatherhood in a nation that professes to be "under God" but refuses to submit to the Word or ways of Father God, both in and out of our churches.[1]

"America is rapidly becoming a fatherless society . . . The importance and influence of fathers has been in significant decline since the Industrial Revolution and is now reaching critical proportions."
—RAY WILLIAMS, EXECUTIVE COACH AND SPEAKER

"There has been a "progressive loss of the father's authority and diminution of his power in the family and over the family."
—ALEXANDER MITSCHERLICH, *SOCIETY WITHOUT A FATHER*

"Fatherlessness is the most harmful demographic trend of our generation."
—DAVID BLANKENHORN, *FATHERLESS AMERICA: CONFRONTING OUR MOST URGENT SOCIAL PROBLEM*

"If present trends continue, the percentage of children living apart from their biological fathers will reach 50% by the next century . . . This massive erosion of fatherhood contributes to many of the major social problems of our time."
—DAVID POPENOE, PROFESSOR OF SOCIOLOGY AT
RUTGERS UNIVERSITY

"Men are losing their grip, opting out, coming apart, and falling behind."
—GUY GARCIA, *THE DECLINE OF MAN*

"A World Without Fathers—The Struggle to Save the Black Family"
—COVER STORY OF *NEWSWEEK*, AUGUST 30, 1993

"The crisis of fatherhood, then, is ultimately a cultural crisis."
—DAVID POPENOE, PROFESSOR OF SOCIOLOGY AT
RUTGERS UNIVERSITY, OP.CIT.

STARTLING CULTURAL STATISTICS

The year 1994 was declared "The Year of the Father" in America as headlined by *Newsweek*, October 31, 1994. Unfortunately, while attempting to bring focus back to fatherhood, it actually served more as a postmortem for fathers. The following cultural indicators reveal why the growing worry.

In 2016, while accepting a best-director Emmy award, Jill Soloway addressed Hollywood, as the culture-defining power of the United States and the Western world, declaring "TOPPLE THE PATRIARCHY!"[2] It was, in effect, a declaration of war against both men and fathers—a repudiation of fatherhood itself. The statistics tell the tale of that revolution that has, in a very real sense, already destroyed the cultural and spiritual foundations of fatherhood. Brace yourself!

The United States is the world's leader in fatherless families. We took over first place from Sweden in 1986.

More than 25 million of America's children do not live with their biological fathers.

In 1960, the number of children living in single-parent families was about 5 million. Today it exceeds 24 million.

No other country has a higher divorce rate than the United States—40 percent of first marriages. That rate was only 16 percent in 1960.

Over 40 percent of children living with their mothers have not seen their fathers in at least a year.

Seventy-two percent of adolescent murderers grew up without fathers in the home.

Sixty percent of America's rapists grew up without fathers.

Seventy percent of incarcerated juveniles grew up without fathers.

Fatherless children are twice as likely to drop out of school.

Fatherless children who exhibit violent behavior are eleven times more likely to do so than those living with both parents.

Seventy-five percent of teen suicides occur in homes where a parent is absent.

Fatherless children are five times more likely to live in poverty than children living with both parents.

Eighty percent of adolescents in psychiatric hospitals come from broken homes.

Over 40 percent of American children are born out of wedlock—approximately 70 percent in the black community.

Roughly 75 percent of American children living without a father will experience poverty before age eleven.

In our nation's capital, only 16 percent of our children live in a home with their father.

The United States is the world's leader in fatherless families.

RESTORING CULTURAL FATHERHOOD

In this chapter we have pulled back the curtain on the cultural follies of fatherlessness. As Asa Baber, in his column, "Men" stated, in response to the publication of *Father* Facts by Dr. Wade Horn, then director of the National Fatherhood Initiative "Those are some of the facts. If we do not change them for the better—and soon—we will not have a society worth living in." Shockingly, that observation was made in 1996, and the deterioration of fatherhood has continued unabated since. Whether we care to admit it or not, we are experiencing a curse—the accumulating curse of fatherlessness. Perhaps the word *folly* itself is foolish at this grave juncture of history in that it insufficiently describes the debacle now destroying both social and spiritual destiny.

Fatherlessness is the most significant family or social problem facing America.

"If it were classified as a disease, fatherlessness would be an epidemic worthy of attention as a national emergency," declared the National Center for Fathering. According to their Fathering in America poll, 72 percent of the U.S. population say "fatherlessness is the most significant family or social problem facing America."[3] Surprisingly, that statistic came from a poll conducted in 1999. And the continuing blatant demeaning of fatherhood since that time now endangers an entire nation. And Americans are transmitting this debaucherous model worldwide.

WHAT MUST WE DO?

There are four simple, though not simplistic, solutions to this demoralizing crisis. These solutions compel us, whether pastor, politician, or simple citizen, to face the facts without attempting to erect walls of self-protecting or group-protecting excuses that serve only to frustrate any and all legitimate efforts to restore fatherhood.

FIRST—The divorce culture now embraced and perpetuated by pastor, politician and people alike must be rejected as fundamentally self-destructive to faith, family, fatherhood and the future.

Divorce is the leading driver of fatherlessness.

This will necessitate legislative policy changes resulting in corresponding legal changes that are driven by dramatic changes in personal convictions among pastors, priests and people. Divorce is the leading driver of fatherlessness and the progressive cultural calamities that rip through our homes and hearts and is the leading cause of poverty. The false compassion driven by the lordship of feelings is destroying fatherhood.

SECOND—Marriage must be restored as the preeminent building block of a stable and joyful nation.

Marriage has been demeaned by free-wheeling divorce attitudes that began with so-called no-fault divorce in 1968, spreading like wildfire throughout America and our churches. When the governors of six Southern states had to declare a "marital emergency" in our country's Bible Belt because their divorce rates had soared beyond those of the nation at large, you know we are in trouble. When Hartford Seminary revealed the divorce rate among pastors to equal that of their parishioners, it should have been clear that pastors are forfeiting the moral authority to speak prophetically, thus, from our pulpits, defining deviancy down.

Marriage was ordained by the Father as the foremost means of displaying the fundamental relationship of Christ the Son to His church . . . the Bride and children of the Father. It should be little wonder that the spiritual attack on marriage should have preceded the calamitous attack on fatherhood. And Christ's "church" has a heavy account to bear as complicit in the carnage, notwithstanding continual cries to the contrary that only perpetuate—indeed, facilitate—the erosion of the foundations of marriage, family and fatherhood.

THIRD—Because marriage alone is the God-ordained relationship in which sex is sanctified by the Father, this spiritual principle must be restored, beginning in the Father's own house.

A generation ago, *U.S. News and World Report* featured a cover story titled "The Trouble with Premarital Sex" (May 19, 1997). Shockingly, a secular and, some would say, liberal newsmagazine dared to deliver a truth that neither pastor nor politician were willing to declare to their constituents. The unabashed conclusion of the article? Adult premarital sex is the "sin" Americans "wink at."[4] But why? It is because it had then, and has now to an even greater extent, become normalized throughout our ostensibly "God-fearing" America.

Key conservative and Christian leaders refused to comment regarding the matter. Why? It is because their own constituencies, from which they derive cultural accolades and financial support, are as deeply enmeshed in this debauchery as their liberal and secular counterparts.

"Why such reticence?" asked the author. The answer: "Americans, at least tacitly, have all but given up on the notion that the appropriate premarital state is one of chastity." Listen carefully! The author was not through:

> The Bible may have warned that, like the denizens of Sodom and Gomorrah, those who give "themselves over to fornication" will suffer "the vengeance of eternal fire" (Jude 7). Yet for most Americans, adult premarital sex has become the "sin" they not only wink at, but quietly endorse.[5]

There are vast social and cultural consequences to unfettered premarital sex. Yet the spiritual consequences are greater still. What of fathers and fathering . . . and fatherhood itself?

How do we hope to somehow restore the hearts of "illegitimate" fathers on earth when even those who *profess* to be Christian are fundamentally disconnected from the heart of the heavenly Father through sexual rebellion?

For most Americans, adult premarital sex has become the "sin" they not only wink at, but quietly endorse.

Please try to follow the Father's passionate plea through the pen of this scrivener.

That same 1997 *U.S. News and World Report* piece warned that, contrary to popular belief, many more adults over twenty years of age than teenagers give birth to kids out of wedlock. "In fact, most of the current social ills tied to sexual behavior . . . stem chiefly from adults who have sex before they marry, not from sexually active teens."[6] Nearly twenty years later, the Associated Press delivered a "reality check" warning of the metastasized cancer that has now invaded the entire culture, including the church.

Consider the metastasizing consequences of the "reality check"—the revelation that 95 percent of all Americans have had premarital sex. Even among those who abstained from sex until age twenty, 80 percent had premarital sex by age forty-four. Is anyone seriously questioning why over 40 percent of all births in this supposed "Christian" nation are out of wedlock (fatherless) and that cohabitation has now surpassed marriage as the "family" foundation of choice?

FOURTH—The psalmist wrote, "If the foundations be destroyed, what can the righteous do?" (Ps. 11:3). The righteous can do only what the righteous alone can do. And what is it that only the righteous have either the understanding or right to do? Only those in right standing on this issue before the Father can, as prophetic voices, declare the absolute truth of our spiritual demise that is defining a nation's destruction.

Genuine compassion, from the Father's heart, demands that we confront the root of the carnage, not with cultural arguments alone, but with piercing prophetic voices declaring the Father's absolute truth, which alone will heal and make us free. Yet *U.S. News and World Report* lamented, "The clergy, once loquacious on the topic of premarital sin, are equally subdued."[7] Religious columnist Michael McManus, in his 1995 book *Marriage Savers*, wrote that "condemnation of adult premarital sex has virtually vanished from religious preaching."[8]

Pastors and parachurch leaders must decide whether to please Father God or to please their increasingly fatherless congregations and constituencies. When *Christianity Today* proclaimed the debauchery rampant in our colleges as "Dorm Brothels" (February 5, 2005), what powerful preaching of righteousness echoed from pulpit to pew? Silence!

When *Christianity Today* in March 2008 proclaimed men in the church to be "Addicted to Sex" in its cover story, what cry of repentance and reconciliation with the Father brought pastor, priest, and fathers to their knees? Silence in the pulpits reveals spiritual complicity with those in the pews. This is not compassion but tacit companionship on a rapidly sinking ship pierced through with spiritual corruption.

The apostle Paul made it plain to a similarly sexually corrupt church: "Be not deceived: neither fornicators, nor idolaters, nor adulterers, nor effeminate, nor abusers of themselves with mankind . . . shall inherit the kingdom of God" (1 Cor. 6:9–10).

CAN WE BE RECONCILED?

The Father is waiting. His merciful hand is reached out still. But it is we who have become prodigal sons. And so the Father's pleading voice echoes through the deepening darkness: "Return unto me, and I will return unto you" (Mal. 3:7).

The spirit of Jezebel has seduced us into her deadly orgy. We have, in this nation proverbially *under God*, sold our souls, pastor and people alike, to the lust of the flesh, and it is reaping corruption. Reveling in unprecedented prosperity, as with ancient Rome, we have abandoned nearly all restraint of the faith of our fathers and have given ourselves wholesale to the unfettered market of our hyper-titillated feelings.

The spirit of Jezebel has seduced us into her deadly orgy.

Can we, who have run into the arms of Jezebel, be restored to relationship with the holy Son of the Father, who is soon to return as our Judge and who will accept only a bride without "spot, wrinkle, or any such thing?" (Eph. 5:27). The answer is yes . . . or no.

Our clue is in Jesus' warning to the church at Thyatira that protected Jezebel: "Except they repent of their deeds, "I will cast her into a bed, *and them that commit adultery with her* into tribulation" (Rev. 2:22). The choice is ours. Repentance will be painful, but the alternative is both temporal destruction and eternal damnation.

Sex is powerful. It will either glorify the Father or engulf us in an orgy of destruction. Raging passion brought annihilation to Sodom and Gomorrah. Unfettered promiscuity destroyed Rome from within. Adultery and fornication (spiritual and physical) divided Israel's heart and brought the wrath of God upon "the apple of His eye." We, like Sodom, Rome and Israel, are poised on the precipice of judgment. "Shall not my soul be avenged on such a nation as this?" asked the Lord (Jer. 5:29).

We the People must decide, beginning in the Father's house: Jesus . . . or Jezebel? Your decision and mine will determine America's destiny . . . and perhaps yours . . . and the destiny of your sons and daughters.

Time is exceedingly short! What we do, we must do quickly!

PROBING OUR HEARTS

1. In what ways is fatherlessness a *curse*?

2. As a father, do you have a deep conviction that this may be your ultimate moment before God? Why . . . or why not?

3. What do you think is included in the term *fatherlessness*? Are there many dimensions or implications of the word?

4. Do you agree that the divorce culture and unwed sexual actions lie at the heart of actual physical fatherlessness? In what way, if any, have you contributed to this cultural crisis?

5. Can fatherlessness be corrected without spiritual repentance? Why or why not?

13

A LASTING LEGACY

Some men build careers. Others erect empires. But the rarest of men leave godly legacies.

—STEVEN LAWSON

EVERY MAN LEAVES A LEGACY. The question, then, is not whether I will leave a legacy, but what the nature and lasting effect of that legacy will be.

THE NATURE OF LEGACY

A legacy is that which a man leaves as a result or outflow of his life. When we hear or use the word *legacy*, we might normally and naturally think of something good or positive issuing from a life. That legacy may be either intentional or unintentional. Unfortunately, however, not all legacies are either good or positive, and some are profoundly perverse.

In the field of law, in which this writer practiced for two decades, use of the word *legacy* normally implies or conjures thoughts of wills or trusts in which tangible real or personal property is parsed to heirs or others one wishes to receive a portion of the decedent's bounty. If such intentions are not precisely declared by will or trust, the state, through laws of intestate succession, will disburse the estate to the "natural objects of your bounty" according to the legislature's best understanding of what you most likely would have intended had you written a will. By will, the legacy (or bequest) is passed on by specific intention. Without a will, the legacy is left to a form of chance, either through negligence in preparation or through procrastination. Procrastination or a cavalier attitude underlies most failure to plan a man's earthly material legacy.

Interestingly, the same patterns of intention and procrastination determine the extent and effect of other potential legacies, which, in the greater scope of both society and spiritual heritage, are of greater value and import, particularly as it relates to fathers. As always, the heart of the matter always lies with our hearts. To what purposes, principles, and ultimate destiny are our fatherly hearts directed? Destiny, yes legacy, lies in the balance of our daily life decisions and direction.

Influence would seem to be our most profound and pervasive legacy.

Influence would seem to be our most profound and pervasive legacy. Influence and life impact occur both by intent and without intent. Our lives influence and impact others, for better or for ill, regardless of our intention. And it is indeed a tragedy that comparatively few men give more than fleeting thoughts to the legacy they are daily defining through actions and attitudes, through decisions and directions that are daily determining the destiny of those in our sphere of influence. Even more tragic is that this pattern prevails among Christian men.

THE TIME VALUE OF LEGACY

The world of finance warns us of what is called "the time value of money." Simply speaking, the earlier a man begins to save or invest during his life, the greater will be the reward at retirement or to his children upon his passing. Consistency is the key.

It is said that "money talks." So, for a moment, we will talk *money*. And it is time that will tell the tale. Time, plus dedicated treasure, yields a financial legacy. But how does the legacy accumulate and truly become a legacy that may last? It is the combination of faithful and disciplined deposits over time plus what is known as "compound interest." Some financial gurus have described the effect of compound interest as "magic."

If we can discover how this "magic" works with money, it will give powerful insight into how our influence today is multiplied many fold so as to leave a life legacy that truly lasts.

Consider these amazing facts of finance. These are simple scenarios to which we can all relate.

FIRST—You want to retire at age 65 with a nest egg of $100,000. Your goal, over time, is to average an annual return of 12 percent. This is the typical rate generated through the stock market over time. To achieve that goal, this is what you will need to contribute:

Beginning at age 25	about $10 per month
Beginning at age 35	about $32 per month
Beginning at age 45	about $109 per month
Beginning at age 55	about 446 per month

Notice, the greater the delay in deciding to make your deposits, the more difficult it becomes to leave the desired legacy or to reach the desired destiny.

SECOND—How can I determine the cost of delaying my decision to set and secure a desired destiny? One thing is certain. None of us can truly afford the high cost of delay. If you saved just $1.00 per day from age 25 at 12 percent average annual interest, you would have $296,516 at age 65. If you wait just one year to begin, you will have $32,000 less at age 65. But if you wait 5 years to begin at age 30, it will cost you $179,000 at age 65, diminishing your nest egg or legacy to only $116,800. Wow! Money really does talk.

Any legacy that will last cannot be left to chance.

Just as most men do not start or even truly consider a disciplined and modest monetary investment early in their adult life, so most men . . . unfortunately even Christian men . . . do not truly consider or begin even modest spiritual investment in their children's lives. Yet the power and effectiveness of that investment early on accumulates through influence, compounding over time so as to leave a genuine and lasting legacy of character, conviction and Christlikeness. Any legacy we truly desire to leave that will last cannot be left to chance. It requires fatherly investment over time.

A LIFE-CHANGING LEGACY

Almost every man wants his life to make a difference. All things considered, in a broad-brush way of thinking or feeling, he wants his life to have some meaningful impact. He wants to believe that in some way his life on earth has had value beyond his mere existence. Yet the fulfillment of such desire is dependent not only on genuine feeling and good intentions but more importantly upon a true and realistic vision coupled with comprehending the components that comprise the greater goal.

Let's look at those primary components. From a secular viewpoint, they are most simply described as *time*, *talent* and *treasure*. There is little question that these three comprise the broader expression and investment of a man's life. Each of these three life legacy components also has a spiritual application and implication without which the "coin" of a man's life is severely diminished in value with a corresponding diminishment or even destruction of desired legacy. It is here that most men fail . . . yes . . . even Christian men.

Failing to see or embrace the profound spiritual implications of legacy, most men, to varying extents, limit their focus and energies to secular expressions and values of time, talent, and treasure because the results seem more immediately measurable or discernable and therefore are more culturally rewarded or praised. Unfortunately, men, desiring to be temporally recognized and rewarded, develop a severe case of spiritual shortsightedness that impairs our ability to impart the greater legacy we would otherwise desire . . . and that God demands. Our Father not only desires but demands that we men, as adopted sons in His family, follow in the footsteps of Jesus, the only begotten Son (John 12:26; 1 Peter 2:21; Phil. 2:5–9; Heb. 12:1–3).

Consider for a moment the profound and enduring legacy of Jesus. Was His legacy predicated on earthly values of time, talent, and treasure, or was (and is) His legacy lasting precisely because He embraced the greater value of the spiritual dimension, realizing that "only one life, 'twill soon be past" and "only what's done for the Father and to please the Father by life investment in His children will last"? That is a man's persistent choice and will determine our ultimate life passion, purpose and legacy.

Perhaps we should then ask, what was it about Jesus' life as a man on earth that enabled Him to both perceive and persist with primary spiritual passion so as to leave a world-changing legacy? Answering that question will likely leave us with important clues as to our own desired legacy . . . a legacy that is life changing.

A CHRIST-INFORMED LEGACY

You and I are admonished to be "followers of God, as dear children" (Eph. 5:1). The word *followers* is best translated from the Greek as "imitators." Since Jesus was sent by the Father to be His "Word made flesh" so that we could experience the Father's ways in real time (see John 1:14), and since Jesus neither spoke nor acted contrary to the Father's will, Jesus then became our example not only for how to live but for how to leave a lasting legacy.

Only true fathers will leave a lasting and godly legacy.

In the following chapter, we will seek to discover the secrets that all men in right relationship with the Father may embrace so as to truly leave a godly legacy. Are you up for the challenge? Only true fathers will leave a lasting and godly legacy.

PROBING OUR HEARTS

1. What does the word *legacy* mean to you?

2. How are the time value of money and spiritual legacy connected?

3. Most men want their lives to make a difference. So . . . what are you doing to leave a lasting impact on your children?

4. In what ways might your life imitate the life of Christ in view of leaving a legacy that will last?

5. What evidence would your children or grandchildren point to in support of a firm belief that your *time*, *talent* and *treasure* belong to the Father?

14

HOW TO LEAVE A GODLY LEGACY

Dads must know the way, show the way, and go the way.

—STEVEN LAWSON

FEW INTENDED LEGACIES LAST. Whether or not a man leaves a legacy worthy of his fatherhood that endures is dependent on the foundation upon which his fatherhood has been built and upon the spiritual "architectural" pattern of his life. In the spiritual portrait of Jesus' life as He related to the Father, we see both the foundation and the building pattern that has defined the legacy of all legacies—a legacy that lasts through the centuries, conquers cultures and transforms the innermost character of citizens to conform to the Father's heart and future home.

WHY DO DESIRED "LEGACIES" NOT LAST?

For good or ill, all of our lives have a lasting effect. It is the component parts of our lives, over time, that set the course of destiny, whether desired or damaging. And so we are told that even God, as Father, "visit[s] the iniquity of the fathers upon the children's children, unto the third and to the fourth generation" (Ex. 34:7; 20:5), and this is true despite the Father's love, long-suffering, and mercy (Num. 14:18).

This should grip the mind and heart of every man, father or father-to-be. It should infuse deep into our spirits the gravamen of God's grace . . . that grace is not extended to overlook or wink at our fatherly failures but rather to encourage and equip us to faithfully follow the Father's "fleshed-out" example, "denying ungodliness and worldly lusts" that "we should live soberly, righteously, and godly, in this present world" (Titus 2:11–14).

Our intended legacies fail because we are seduced by failing worldly patterns.

Our intended legacies fail because we follow or are seduced by failing worldly patterns or by the persistent power of our flesh, which commands us incessantly to do things our own way. A lasting legacy for which most yearn is built over time and upon the foundation of truth. Since Jesus declared, "I am *the* way, *the* truth, and *the* life" (John 14:6), perhaps we should take a closer look at His life, from which we can draw inspiration for leaving a lasting, godly legacy.

A TWO-TIERED LEGACY

The natural mind of man after the fall of Adam is set to a

carnal or secular default. The viewpoint of men, even ostensibly "Christian" men, drifts consistently to an earth-based, here-and-now mode, or what seems right in the short-term mentality. And it is this pervasive "default" orientation that sets the stage for what we see as valuable in terms of both our thinking and our decisions. It defines where and how we spend our time, invest our resources, and devote our talents. After all, we do live in this present world.

The problem is that we were created in the Father's image as spiritual sons, living in an otherwise secular world. When the secular predominates over the spiritual, we lose the Father's perspective, resulting in a profound shift away from His will and ways. In this way, our desired godly legacies become perverted, undermined and even destroyed. The entire history of mankind, yes even biblical history of purported followers of the Father, portrays this painful reality.

Enter Jesus—the Father's only begotten Son, full of both *grace* AND *truth*. Jesus reset and redefined this historical default system that persistently fell back on a secular viewpoint for survival and sense of purpose. Rather, He revived the lordship of the spiritual legacy over the secular, declaring, "My meat [food] is to do the will of Him that sent me, and to finish his work" (John 4:34). And His parables continually provoked the hearer to see things from the Father's perspective . . . *if* they had eyes to see, ears to hear, and hearts yearning to understand.

"IF YOU HAVE SEEN ME . . ."

So then how did Jesus, as the Son, reveal in and through His life what the Father's expected intentions were for all who would follow in Jesus' footsteps? How are we to leave a legacy that lasts for eternity rather than some limited, earthbound, temporally defined memory or money?

Perhaps the secret lies in Jesus' own words:

"my Father is greater than I." (John 14:28)

"I love the Father: and as the Father gave me commandment, even so I do." (John 14:31)

"He that hath seen me hath seen the Father; so how can you say, 'Show us the Father'?" (John 14:9)

"If a man love me, he will keep my words: and my Father will love him, and we will come unto him and make our abode with him." (John 14:23)

"If you have seen me," said Jesus, "you have seen the Father." If that be true, what, then, have we seen in the life of Christ that should reset our Adamic default system, produced by the Fall, from predominantly secular and temporal to that which will produce a lastingly spiritual legacy? Let's explore that by looking at twelve simple yet simply profound principled practices.

PATTERN OF THE PATRIARCH

Remember the Hollywood celebrity in chapter 11 who provoked the spirit of any man aspiring to a godly legacy by declaring passionately on national television, "Topple the patriarchy!"?[1] Not only is this a poisoning cry of two generations that have forsaken the fear of the Lord, but is a reflection, in a more religiously camouflaged way, of the feminization of fatherhood in our churches and the defiling of God the Father in our increasingly immoral imaginations.

Jesus reset the pattern to establish the role of a patriarch on this planet while we await the culmination of all things. As He said, "If you have seen me, you have seen the Father." "So . . . what did Jesus see and do that fundamentally set His course such that He would leave the Father's intended legacy through His life?

1. JESUS FEARED!

This is the absolute foundation for any godly man or father, yet today both pastor and people tend to flee from this foundation. We must ask ourselves why. Why do we see the full "fear of the Lord" as offensive both to our culture and to those who purport to embrace Jesus as Lord and Messiah? Have we submitted to the ways of our culture rather than to the ways of Christ?

Why do we see the "fear of the Lord" as offensive?

Consider well! Isaiah, in foretelling the coming of the Messiah and describing His life and ministry, declared:

> And the spirit of the LORD shall rest upon him, the spirit of wisdom and understanding, the spirit of counsel and might, the spirit of knowledge and of *the fear of the LORD*; and shall make him of quick understanding in *the fear of the LORD*. (Isa. 11:2–3)

What man, purporting to embrace God as Father, does not inwardly desire that the spirit of the Lord rest upon him, that he be blessed with the spirit of wisdom and understanding—of counsel and might—of godly knowledge? So we must ask, why have these desirable attributes of patriarchy so eluded men both past and present? It is because of the missing quintessential foundation upon which *all* such blessings and attributes are based—the *fear of the Lord*.[2]

2. JESUS SOUGHT, LISTENED, AND READ

"Blessed are they that *hear* the word of God, and keep it," declared Jesus (Luke 11:28). "Take heed what ye *hear*," He taught, so that "unto you that *hear* shall more be given" (Mark 4:24). True hearing was at the heart of Jesus' legacy.

Jesus warned those who *claimed* to be believers, heirs according to the promise to Abraham, of being "dull of hearing," revealing a stubborn and closed heart unable or unwilling to produce a goodly and godly heritage (Matt. 13:15). "By hearing ye shall hear, and shall not understand," He lamented (Matt. 13:14). Not only did Jesus warn of *what* we hear but also of *how* we hear (Luke 8:18).

Jesus' ear was tuned to the Father's frequency. He had highly selective hearing, both as to *what* He heard and *how* He heard it. And so we, as fathers, must ask rhetorically, "What do I hear and how do I hear it?" What do I allow into the ear gate of my heart that defines how I think and the values I pass on?

And more importantly, is my ear tuned to the Father's frequency—His heart, His expectations, His Word? Does His Word register deeply on the membranes of my mind, or does it pass in one ear and out the other without producing the fruit of the Father's heart?

True *hearing* also requires reading. Jesus knew His Father's Word because He purposed to read it and absorb it into the deepest membranes of His mind, thus defining and directing His thoughts, enabling Him to speak with authority rather than merely informationally. It was His custom (Luke 4:16, 32, 36). Yet most men today resist reading.

Jesus said nothing but what He first heard from the Father, thus enabling Him as the Son to speak transformationally with true authority. And for this reason and to this end He frequently sought special time away with His Father so that the clamor and cultural noise would not adulterate their heart communications (Matt. 14:23; Luke 6:12; Mark 1:35). Are we more prone to seek the voice of the culture or the voice of Christ, who has heard the Father. How would we know? What is the probative testimony of your innermost thoughts? Do we really want to leave a godly legacy that will last?

3. JESUS WATCHED AND OBSERVED

What am I watching? What am I importing into my spirit through the eye gate of my mind? What do I see and observe that tends to dominate my decisions and direction? How do I interpret and factor in what I choose to see that may be unwittingly defining not only my destiny but those who are following after me?

Jesus made clear that "the Son can do nothing of himself, but what He seeth the Father do: for what things soever He doeth, these also doeth the Son likewise. For the Father loveth the Son, and showeth Him all things that himself doeth" (John 5:19–20).

The obvious question, then, is "Do I spend sufficient time with the Father, with a listening ear, such that I can hear His still, small voice and emulate what He is doing? And do I have sufficient dedicated, relational and quiet presence with my children that they can both *feel* and *follow* my life and leading? These are provocative challenges amid the cacophony of our overwhelmingly noisy and demanding carnal culture.

4. JESUS FOLLOWED AND IMITATED

Whose will do I follow? What would be the testimony of my sons and daughters . . . my wife . . . my grandchildren?

Jesus declared, "I seek not my own will, but the will of the Father which hath sent me" (John 5:30). Do I truly seek the Father's will, or do I more likely seek for the Father to put His blessing upon my own will?

Because Jesus so willingly and observably followed the Father's will, He, in effect, became an imitator of the Father. Therefore, the apostle Paul enjoins us all, "Be ye therefore followers [imitators] of God, as dear children," and walk as Christ the Son walked, not defined by the earmarks of the world around us in which we are immersed (Eph. 5:1–12). When we imitate the ways of the carnal culture, we actually are bringing "the wrath of God [the Father] upon [us as] the children of disobedience" (Eph. 5:6). And this wrath echoes progressively through our own lives to invade and ultimately defile our desired legacy.

5. JESUS SUBMITTED

It is one thing to know the Father's will, but it is quite another to willingly submit to it. As men and fathers, we continually face this destiny-determining choice. And it is a matter of my will.

James, the brother of Jesus, well understood our dilemma, admonishing us to "submit [ourselves] therefore to God. Resist the devil, and he will flee from you" (James 4:7). Is it not true that our tendency is only to "resist the devil" rather than to truly "submit to God" as our Father? Our pride in this regard actually causes the Father to resist us and withdraw His grace that we most desperately need (v. 6). Yet it is God [the Father] who yearns to "[work] in you both to will and to do of his good pleasure" (Phil. 2:13).

How can I expect my children to submit to my will when I refuse to submit to the will of my Father?

Jesus well understood the necessity of submission of His will to that of His Father, declaring "…I seek not my own will, but the will of the Father which hath sent me" (John 5:30).

And so, a probing question echoes to us in our generation. How can I expect my children to submit to *my* will when I refuse to submit to the will of my Father? My legacy hangs on the line of my observable pattern of submitting or yielding to the Father's will. How, then, is that pattern of submission of my will revealed?

6. JESUS OBEYED

The sole proof of submission to the Father's will is *obedience*. Yet, as we have already seen, the very word *obey* is anathema to most of the twenty-first-century church. How can this be? We are, in effect, cutting off the most essential operational lifeline to a godly legacy.

Obedience reveals the genuineness of professed love. Jesus well understood this. First, Jesus, as a Son, "became obedient by the things that he suffered." Because of that obedience, "he became the author of eternal salvation unto all them that *obey* Him" (Heb. 5:8–9).

Faithful obedience to the Father and the Son is the ultimate expression of love leading to a lasting legacy. "If a man love me," said Jesus, "he will keep my words [obey God]: and my Father will love him, and we will come unto him, and make our abode with him" (John 14:23, see also 1 John 5:2–3).

Just imagine the legacy of loving obedience taking root both in your children and grandchildren and in this generation, preparing for the second coming of our Lord. Would it not usher in a season of "joy unspeakable and full of glory" (1 Peter 1:8)? Can you fathom the incredible satisfaction of such fruit of fatherhood?

7. JESUS FELLOWSHIPPED

Just as fathers yearn for the undefinably satisfying fellowship with their sons, daughters and grandchildren, even so children deeply desire the same undefinably satisfying fellowship with their fathers. Jesus was no different. Yet such fellowship seems almost eternally elusive. So, again, we must ask ourselves, "Why?"

Unfortunately, neither fathers nor their offspring seem to truly comprehend the sheer joy of such fellowship that awaits them . . . if only. And the word *if* is the biggest little word in the Bible. All blessing—and eternal salvation itself—hangs on the little word *if*, as in "If my people . . ." (2 Chron. 7:14). If we want to leave a legacy that lasts, with joy, we must capture the essence of the great and seemingly elusive *if*. Jesus modeled its essence, both in heaven and on earth.

A few windows into Jesus' fellowship with the Father should suffice, at least to sow the seeds that will produce the fruit of such fellowship in our lives, leaving a deep and enduring legacy.

First, Jesus purposed as Son to spend quality time with His Father, in full confidence that the Father was always available . . . never too busy. But in order to do that, He knew that He had to get away from the incessant demands and noise of the surrounding culture and even of His calling, because fellowship with His Father was the foundation for all else he was doing . . . or would do (Luke 5:16; 6:12). Such relationship is built, not on sperm donorship or even on professed belief in the Father or the Son, but on genuine relational and heart-uniting time together, focusing not on peripheral matters but on the things that matter most.

Second, Jesus made His Father's will His own will. In that way, son's and father's hearts were united in agreement as one heart (John 5:30). It should not seem a mystery, then, that if my son and daughter perceive that my will is inconsistent with the Father's will, their own wills will be at dissonance with my will as a father, thus impeding or undermining the depth of fellowship I so much desire.

"This is my beloved Son, in whom I am well pleased" (Matt. 17:5). Words of a living legacy that few sons and daughters ever hear from their fathers.

Third, the Father affirmed the Son, both privately and publicly, declaring, "This is my beloved Son, in whom I am well pleased; hear ye him" (Matt. 17:5). Powerful words! These are the words of a living legacy that few sons and daughters ever hear from their fathers. When spoken publicly, they are frequently only falsely motivated words of pride so as to build up the father. But when spoken both privately (with deep sincerity) and with corresponding public affirmation, they become words of great power and holy purpose.

8. JESUS LOVED

Love is a reciprocating experience, yet it is born out of the depth of fundamental relationship. A father who does not display the drama of sacrificial love for his son will not likely experience the desired depth of reciprocity from his son. And the joyful relationship that could have been born and blossomed gradually languishes, with both father and his children wondering why. Feet must be put to alleged faith.

Love that breeds a lasting joyful legacy demands continual loving investment with an ultimate view to the legacy it will produce that will live on to the next and future generations. And so it was . . . and is . . . with Jesus and the Father.

Jesus spoke passionately about His reciprocating love with His Father. "For the Father," He said, "loveth the Son, and sheweth him all things that himself doeth" (John 5:20). With confidence Jesus could then declare, "He that honoureth not the Son honoureth not the Father" (v. 23). Why then do many men purport to honor the Son, but the Father, not quite so much . . . especially when Jesus made clear "If you have seen Me, you have seen the Father"? Could it be that, even as Christian fathers, we do not much *like*, let alone *love*, the Father? And if that be even partially true, might it also be that our refusal to embrace the Father in full love becomes a barrier in our relationship with our sons and daughters, preventing them from embracing us fully, with total conviction deep in their spirits of our complete love for them?

Here is the crux of our love, noted Jesus: "As the Father hath loved me, so I have loved you: [so] continue ye in my love. *If* ye keep my commandments, ye shall abide in my love; even as I have kept my Father's commandments, and abide in his love" (John 15:9–10). Genuine love, from God's viewpoint, is rooted in a continuing legacy of obedience . . . a father's obedience first to the Father, which becomes progressively reflected in the children's loving obedience toward their own fathers and grandfathers. That is spelled L-E-G-A-C-Y!

9. JESUS ENDURED

Life is not a bed of roses. It can be tough at times, and tougher yet at other times. And our sons and daughters need to be taught loving toughness both by precept and example. As we see the prophesied terrifying and troubled times shortly preceding Christ's second coming approaching—even knocking at our doors—the time has come for fathers to impart perseverance and endurance to their children.

True biblical love requires a special kind of godly toughness. Yet as the feminization of both culture and church advances, it seems there is little stomach for fathers to develop such fortitude in their own lives, let alone in the lives of their children. So how did Jesus do it, and why?

True biblical love requires a special kind of godly toughness.

Endurance and perseverance were deeply ingrained in Jesus' mind, heart and ministry. Their root was in a profound sense of both calling and obedience. And so He warned His spiritual sons (disciples) that "he that shall endure unto the end, the same shall be saved" (Matt. 24:13; Mark 13:13). And as to His own perseverance, He "endured the cross . . . for the joy [legacy] that was set before him." (So we, as spiritual sons and daughters, beginning with fathers, are to "Consider him . . . lest ye be wearied and faint in your minds." For that reason, we fathers are to "run with patience the race that is set before us, looking unto Jesus," who set the example (Heb. 12:1–3). This is necessarily tough talk for these troubled times . . . if we desire to leave a legacy that lasts.

A short and recent personal story may help to give the deeper implications of endurance and perseverance. Lessons learned in the flesh transfer, when applied, to our spiritual lives.

A few years ago, I was passionately moved to provide just such a test of perseverance and endurance for my oldest grandsons, who were then thirteen, fifteen, and nineteen, all brothers. I began to prepare them for a mini expedition to climb a fourteen-thousand-foot glaciated peak in the Sierra Nevada mountains that would take us across the country to vistas unknown to them. The ascent would take us from approximately eight thousand feet elevation to the summit, a gain of six thousand vertical feet over ten miles of switch-backing trails before the final climb to the pinnacle.

Special boots, equipment and clothing were acquired so as to meet every anticipated eventuality. We all acted to prepare physically and mentally. And then we began the "assault" on our goal. Mile after dogged mile we lifted ever-heavier boots and packs, often thirsty and with increasing bone weariness, until, at long last, we reached the saddle at twelve thousand feet, where we would pitch our tents for the summit bid in the morning. All was then glorious. Anticipation was high! And then it happened.

With a sixty-pound pack on my back, I slipped and fell backward and downward eight feet, badly twisting my left knee, tearing both the medial meniscus in front and the anterior cruciate ligament behind, painfully preventing our final ascent—a glorious summit victory.

Rest provided no recovery and so we began our treacherous evening descent—benighted and desperately bedraggled—headlamps revealing the gravest dangers—until arriving at a temporary campsite at 11:00 p.m.

Morning was not glorious! Swelling, debilitating pain, and instability forced a makeshift knee brace, and the remaining four-thousand-foot descent loomed ahead.

A doctor, seeing our plight, declared, "This is epic!" Mercifully, he supplied a dose of pain medication. And we proceeded down, grandsons having divided up my heavy pack, increasing their heavy burdens to the breaking point. They begged me to call for an airlift. We encountered a pack train, but the pack master declined to help, declaring it far too dangerous in light of the terrain and my serious disability.

And onward we trudged. No strides—only a painful shuffle protected by ice ax and hiking sticks. Tough young grandsons were reduced to tears with the burden of a debilitated papa and their own pain under the now unmercifully heavy loads. Everything in me . . . and them . . . screamed to quit—to give up. Together we suffered and endured, and the memories are indelibly fixed as the years have passed—that only those who endure to the end . . . who persevere in the face of intense struggle, remaining true to the cause, shall be saved.

The undergirding purpose for which I inaugurated this *expedition* was to teach, through experience, the very lessons of perseverance in the clutches of life's challenges that now had exploded on steroids in our life together. I knew, and they now viscerally understand, that the only way to learn endurance is to experience the screaming need for it, often in the most adverse of circumstance, as did Jesus. And Papa . . . or fathers . . . must show the way. The painful memories have somewhat waned, and my grandsons, for the anticipated joy set before them, now desire to go again for another summit bid, as do I. But the transferable concept of that experience has strengthened them in observable ways to endure the challenges of life they continue to face.

Our children are waiting for men to become fathers who champion enduring faith . . . to the end.

As the coach famously said, "When the going gets tough, the tough get going." And dads and grandfathers must pave the way, because the spiritual challenges ahead for our sons and daughters will supremely confront their natural ability to cope in ways almost unprecedented in human history. Are you up for the challenge? Our children are waiting for men to become fathers who champion enduring faith . . . to the end.

10. JESUS LOOKED BEYOND HIMSELF

"Where there is no vision, the people perish" (Prov. 29:18). For many men, the very concept of vision is limited to anticipating weekends, vacations and retirement . . . or ball games. But if this is the extent of our primary vision, defined by such often elusive dreams and minuscule, temporally defined hopes, our children and grandchildren will be destined for great disappointment.

Jesus well understood the human tendency to place inordinate value on the temporal. He, like us, had to resist the fleshly draw to relatively valueless pursuits that would inevitably compromise the greater purpose for His life. And so must we if we are to leave a legacy that will truly last. Remember, Jesus was tempted in all manner as we are, yet He set our example to follow the Father and His will as the greatest of all life hope and investment (John 5:30; Heb. 4:15).

We would do well to remember Esau. Esau was willing to sacrifice the greater hope and promise of God's intended purpose for temporal satisfaction (Gen. 25:27–34). Rather than inheriting a blessing, his choice became our eternal curse, not only for him but for all his descendants. His brother, Jacob, however, had the greater vision passed down from father Abraham, through Isaac, to Jacob, whose name was ultimately changed to Israel. Notice the line of blessing by embracing an eternal vision for your sons and grandsons . . . and Jesus was the distant inheritor of the blessing . . . the only obedient son of Israel.

"Jacob have I loved," said the Father, "but Esau have I hated"

(Rom. 9:13; see also Mal. 1:2–3). It was not Esau's person, as made in the image of the Father, that God hated. Rather it was his immensely foolish and shortsighted choices that defiled and desecrated the destiny of his progeny, thus destroying a potentially godly legacy.

And so we must rhetorically enquire of ourselves, "Am I a Jacob or an Esau?" Jesus was a "Jacob" and set our example. What example are you, are we, am I setting?

11. JESUS TAUGHT

Jesus taught by precept and by example. Interestingly, Jesus spent little time *informing* either His twelve disciples or the others who followed Him as potential spiritual sons and daughters. Rather, His teaching was transformative . . . always applicational.

Fathers make a huge mistake thinking that by merely teaching biblical information they are fulfilling the Father's serious and commanded expectation that His Word be presented primarily with profound and life-changing application. As I repeat often on *Viewpoint*, our national radio program available daily at saveus.org, "Information without transformation leads to frustration, stagnation, and often termination."

The Father has not called us to be *informed*, but rather to be *transformed* "by the renewing of [our] mind[s] that [we] may prove what is that good, and acceptable, and perfect, will of God" (Rom. 12:2). The bridge between information and transformation is pointed *application*. Unfortunately, many pastors, supposed spiritual fathers, fail grievously in making precise, genuine, transformative application, thus either depriving or even deceiving those who are trusting their *fathering* role.

In this way, our entire country has become progressively

biblically ignorant, resulting in dire moral and spiritual deterioration. As the apostle Paul so aptly described:

> When for the time ye ought to be teachers, ye have need that one teach you again which be the first principles of the oracles of God; and are become such as have need of milk and not of strong meat.
>
> For every one that useth milk is unskillful in the word of righteousness: for he is a babe. (Heb. 5:12–13)

It was said of Jesus, "…He taught them as one having authority, and not as the scribes" (Matt. 7:29). For that reason they were "astonished" at His teaching (Mark 1:22). Jesus did not teach religiously or as a catechism of religious information, as did the pastors or religious leaders of the day. Rather, He spoke or taught transformatively, and the people readily discerned the difference.

And so it will be with your children and grandchildren. They readily discern the difference. Teaching mere biblical information destines them to perpetual spiritual babyhood, incapable of spiritual maturity, thereby dramatically suppressing any desired legacy.

Teaching mere biblical information destines perpetual spiritual babyhood.

So . . . what must I do in order to speak with authority—not institutional authority but genuine relational authority gleaned from the Father? I must do exactly what Jesus did.

Jesus meditated on the Father's Word daily, with purpose.

Jesus withdrew daily to be with His Father, even if it meant very early before sunrise.

Jesus listened to His Father, daily, and followed what the Father said.

Jesus persisted, despite fleshly feelings to the contrary, to obey and do the precise will of the Father, without excuse.

Jesus cared so much for His disciples and the others who followed Him that He was willing to tell them the whole truth, even if they might no longer follow Him . . . or even mock Him.

12. JESUS PROMISED

Promises, promises. How many fathers and grandfathers make promises . . . and then do not keep them? How does such persistent failure to keep promises affect the trust of the children in their fathers? And how does such failure, whether intentional or negligent, affect the ability of our sons and daughters to place their absolute trust in their heavenly Father? Is it not sowing the seeds of distrust deep in the subconscious minds of those we were hoping to mentor to follow the Master?

True! We all fail to keep promises from time to time as imperfect men, either forgetting the promises we make or rationalizing why we should not keep them, believing our failure to have little or no lasting consequence. Yet lurking silently in those failures is the progressive demise of desired trust, undermining the faith of our supposed followers, unwittingly compromising their faith in the Father, until a legacy of true faith goes the way of all flesh to lamentable destruction of the legacy we hoped to leave.

Jesus, on the other hand, well knew the power of promises . . . promises fulfilled. He deeply and consciously embraced the significance of the hope residing in a promise . . . and that such promise must be carefully made and kept. He was profoundly impressed with the understanding that He represented the Father, that the Father had made covenantal promises both to men and peoples, and that the Father would neither forget nor fail to keep His promises. And so, Jesus made clear, "He that hath seen Me, hath seen the Father" (John 14:9).

Wow!!! Just imagine. Jesus was totally convinced, even though He was born of woman in the flesh, that He not only represented the Father in a broad or generic way, but that His word must be as dependable as that of His Father. And we, as men and fathers, are called to follow in Jesus' steps, faithfully keeping our word, as revealed continually in our actions.

As Paul the apostle stated, "All the promises of God" the Father are "yea" and "amen" in Christ Jesus (2 Cor. 1:20). Jesus, the incarnation or embodiment of the Father's word, became the Word fleshed out, full of both grace and truth (John 1:14). (John 1:14). A God of truth keeps His promises precisely because what He says is the truth and can be depended upon.

What legacy am I leaving as a result of speaking the truth and keeping my promises?

The haunting question then hovers over our lives as fathers: What legacy am I leaving as a result of my practice of both speaking the truth and keeping my promises? We may not be perfect, but perhaps we should be more attuned to our seeming passive influence and therefore press more faithfully to the mark for the high calling the Father has given us. Let us, who are pressing on to perfection as Jesus requires, be thus minded (Phil. 3:13–14), leaving a godly legacy.

PROBING OUR HEARTS

1. Why is it that intended legacies usually do not last?

2. As a Christian man, are there ways in which the worldly culture has seduced you away from a life of spiritual integrity?

3. Do you have any sense that your fatherhood is under assault? From what sources do you perceive the assault pressing upon you?

4. Was there anything about the life of Christ that stands out to you, in particular, as related to becoming a *patriarch*?

5. What legacy do you think you are leaving based upon your practice of both *speaking the truth* and *keeping your promises*?

15

WHEN FATHERS FAIL

The family is a seminary of the church and nation.
—JAMES LANGLOIS, THE FAMILY BIBLE REVOLUTION

EVERY FATHER FAILS at some time and in some way. We all fail, to some degree, in both attitude and action. Perfect fatherhood, on earth, is a goal rather than an achievement, a desire rather than a defined destiny, a hope rather than a guaranteed heritage. Yet, despite our failures, faithfully lived fatherhood is both fulfilling in our time and leaves a legacy for all time.

How can such comparative imperfection leave a lasting legacy of holy purpose and godly heritage? Is this yet another mystery of the Father's ways for us to more deeply explore and also embrace?

THE MYSTERY OF FATHERHOOD

Many of the most profound truths of Scripture are declared to be *mysteries*. We touched on this briefly in chapter 4. First there is the "mystery of God" (Rev. 10:7). Then there are the "mysteries of the kingdom of heaven" (Matt. 13:11), the "mystery of the kingdom of God" (Mark 4:11), the mystery of the Gentile believers being grafted into the original olive tree of Israel (Rom. 11:25) and the "mystery of Christ" (Eph. 3:4). Yet the mysteries continue.

The "mystery of the gospel" itself makes clear there is something about the gospel yet to be fully understood and embraced so as to comprehend and experience its glory (Eph. 6:19). By contrast, we are warned of the "mystery of iniquity" (2 Thess. 2:7) and the mystery of the resurrection (1 Cor. 15:51). The apostle Paul admitted that he spoke "the wisdom of God in a mystery" (1 Cor. 2:7) and that God, the Father, makes "known unto us the mystery of his will" through Christ (Eph. 1:9).

It all sounds so *mysterious*, doesn't it? And yet the *mysterious* nature of things spiritual, from the Father's viewpoint, reveals that we fathers, who purport to be *spiritual* as sons of God in our generation, might well give further consideration that, as with everything else of the kingdom of God, the very nature of our fatherhood also bears the mark of *mystery*.

Perhaps it is easier for us fathers to comprehend the broader and unperceived scope and value of our fatherhood more clearly when we hear the Father's view of marriage. Marriage and fatherhood are two of the foundational *institutions* of the Father's plan and purpose for both the civil and spiritual functions of His creation. For this reason, Paul described his teaching regarding marriage, both civil and spiritual, as "a great mystery"

(Eph. 5:32), for it reveals, in its fullness, the relationship of Christ and His church.

Fatherhood bears the marks of a great mystery.

By implication, then, fatherhood itself bears the marks of a great mystery that the Father of our Lord Jesus Christ desires that we not only understand but make real how we view our role as fathers. Just as our failure to understand this *mystery* regarding our marriages has resulted in massive undermining of marriage in our generation, so too has our failure to understand and embrace the powerful mystery of fatherhood, resulting in a similar catastrophic demise of true fatherhood.

Consider the consequences of our failure to seek and embrace these mysteries if, indeed, we are on the near edge of Christ's second coming. For we are forewarned: Christ is not coming back for a church "having spot, wrinkle or any such thing; but that it should be holy and without blemish" (Eph. 5:27).

WHY FATHERS FAIL

While we must come to understand the *mystery* of fatherhood, the reasons for our failure are not at all mysterious. Rather, our failures are rooted in a rather visionless, shortsighted outlook on life. There are four main reasons most Christian fathers are destined to otherwise unnecessary levels of failure. Let's consider them briefly.

1. FAILURE TO EMBRACE THE FUTURE NOW

The future is always NOW. It begins NOW, not tomorrow, not next week, not next month or next year.

The future does not begin after I graduate or get some degree. It does not begin after my business is established or after a level of financial savings appear to secure the future of my family. Neither does the future begin after the sports season that so attracts me is done. Excuses always lie ahead and multiply like rabbits, continually enabling me to rationalize waiting for the next *best* season, which never seems to materialize.

The future is always NOW, not next month or next year.

The future begins NOW . . . *TODAY*. Perhaps we might mentally imagine a life bumper sticker defining our viewpoint on fathering—DECISION TODAY—DESTINY TOMORROW.

2. FAILURE TO INVEST NOW FOR THE FUTURE

If I clearly see that the future begins NOW, by logical implication, that which I do . . . or fail to do . . . as it relates to defining future destiny and lasting legacy must also begin NOW.

Procrastination is neither good nor godly and inevitably leads to grave consequences. I am a father today and must therefore begin a godly legacy of my fatherhood TODAY, not tomorrow. Remember: "Today was tomorrow yesterday."

How many months or years do I have that I might turn my heart fully to the Father so that the hearts of my children may be turned fully both to the Father and to me as His surrogate? As prophecy and history rapidly become as one, our time is clearly and convincingly NOW.

3. FAILURE TO SEE THE FUTURE POWER OF PRESENT WAYS

Since the future begins today, hope also arises from the decisions and directions established today. Most would, at least in concept, agree. But life in Christ must move quickly from concept or even confession to real life application.

Failure to leave a godly legacy lies in the lurch between spiritual theory and transformational spiritual living. I must come to absolute conviction, as a father or grandfather, or as a spiritual *father*, that my present godly ways are the engine the Father uses to define and power His desired legacy for my life. To the extent I fail to act by faith to conform my attitudes and actions to the ways of the Father today, I compromise my desired legacy tomorrow.

4. FAILURE TO "CONNECT THE DOTS" BETWEEN LIFE AND LEGACY

There is a nearly straight line between the way I live my life and the legacy I leave.

As men and fathers, we all know our propensity to ratio-nalize the choices we make, justifying unrighteous actions, attitudes and decisions as being relatively insignificant in the direction of our lives and the impact they make on those around us. Yet it is the godly continuity of our lives in ways seemingly small or great that actually, in the end, define who we are and the legacy we will leave.

We must resist persistently the temptation to disconnect the decisions we make today from the looming reality of a destiny being defined in the minds and hearts of those we say we love. Indeed, the future is defined by the reality of my living faith today.

REVERSING FATHERLY FAILURE

While fatherly failure is universal, it, like all other aspects of our lives, is a matter of degree. The degree of failure is most often defined by the extent to which we do not appreciate or activate the profound nature and implications of the *mystery* of fatherhood.

Mysteries are characterized as such not just because they are not currently known or understood but also because they beckon us to search them out so as to resolve the *mystery*. That is our Father's intention regarding all of the *mysteries* of His Kingdom and ways. And where aspects of the mystery reside solely with God, we then, as sons, must then yield to the seemingly undisclosed fullness of the Father's will and ways. These are the two essentials to reversing fatherly failures, and they cannot be circumvented.

Once I, as a father, resolve that I must truly seek out the Father's greater understanding and perspective concerning fatherhood, and then determine to yield obediently, without resistance to what is revealed, resting in His overarching desire to bless the world through my own seemingly limited fatherly efforts, I must then turn my heart and I will bear fruit as that which seemed mysterious begins to unfold.

I MUST DESIRE

Fatherly failure will never be reversed without sincere desire. It is a desire to change the current pattern leading to a destiny that I clearly do not desire for my children and to avoid judgment that may come upon me for stubbornly refusing to change.

Fatherly failure will never be reversed without sincere desire.

I MUST DECIDE

Regardless of how far I have fallen short, I must decide to embrace the mystery of the Father's ways and purposes, trusting that He will progressively reveal the *mystery* in due time and in due season, if I faint not.

Such decision requires first admitting any failure as a father, both to God and to my children, seeking their forgiveness. That is *confession*.

Secondly, I must turn from my casual and worldly defined approach to fathering to embrace the Father's greater mystery of fathering, which will, over time, define a lasting spiritual legacy. That is *repentance*. I must declare, both to the Father and to my children and spouse, my commitment before God and ask for their prayerful support.

I MUST DETERMINE

It is one thing to desire, another thing to decide, yet quite another thing to follow through with that which I have decided. This is where most resolutions fail.

Determination means that my mind and heart must be united so as to do what I mentally intended to do. This is the reason why it is said, "The road to hell is paved with good intentions."

Good intentions alone do not please the Father any more than the protested good intentions of our sons and daughters please us as fathers when they do not follow through with our instructions. It is for this reason we are admonished, "Be ye doers of the word, and not hearers only, deceiving your own selves" (James 1:22). We rationalize that because we desired to be good fathers and intended to be, therefore we should be credited with having been good fathers. It is this mind-set that has largely led to the radical breakdown of both fatherhood in general and fatherly authority in particular.

Good intentions alone do not please the Father.

I must determine to *be* a godly father, and that determination must frame my *ministry* as a father and determine my daily decisions. It becomes, then, a major and guiding meditation of my heart, knowing that I am aligning myself in spirit and in truth with the Father's will. Freedom, faith, and joyful fatherhood follow in the wake of such determination.

I MUST BE DILIGENT

If I truly desire to be a godly father, decide to do so and determine to press toward that mark, I must do so with diligence.

Diligence is a corollary to perseverance. I must press toward the mark, and then keep on pressing without relenting. How many well-intentioned fathers become jazzed after a message or seminar, determined to follow through and to genuinely become that godly father their heart desires to be, but fail yet again after neglecting to diligently pursue and practice the attitudes and actions that the Father has so clearly described and revealed in His Word?

There is a reason why the apostle Peter admonished us to "give diligence to make [our] calling and election sure" (2 Peter 1:10). We are also called to "keep [our] heart with all diligence" (Prov. 4:23) and to "look diligently lest any man fail of the grace of God" (Heb. 12:15). Grace is God's part; diligence is our part.

I MUST DELIGHT IN THE FATHER'S WILL

Determination and diligence is not drudgery for a truly godly father. Rather, he delights to do the Father's will, realizing daily that he both pleases the Father and is promising a blessed legacy for his progeny.

If we will delight ourselves in doing as our Father desires, not only will we likely see serious fruit from our labors in this life, but we can also anticipate the eternal blessing of the Father declaring "Well done, my good and faithful servant [father]: thou hast been faithful . . . Enter thou into the joy of thy Lord" (Matt. 25:21).

THE FUTURE AFTER FAILURE

All of us as fathers have failed in one way or another. Most of us lament to some degree our failures. But failure need not define the future.

Today is the first day of the rest of your life.

The future begins today. As it is written, "*Today* if you will hear His voice, harden not your hearts" (Heb. 3:7). The choice is ours. If we will, by faith, make the choices that will leave a lasting godly heritage, God, by His Spirit, will enable us to make the necessary changes.

Remember this: today is the first day of the rest of your life.

PROBING OUR HEARTS

1. In what ways does fatherhood bear the mark of *mystery*?

2. Were you able to see yourself in any of the four ways fathers tend to fail? Describe . . . reflect.

3. Did you find yourself challenged in any way by the points discussed for reversing fatherly failure?

4. Have you made any decisions to reverse patterns of fatherly failure? What are those decisions?

5. Why do you think it is so difficult for men to both see and accept that the future begins today and to make changes accordingly?

16

FALSE FATHERS

The father to the children shall make known thy truth.

—ISAIAH 38:19

FALSE FATHERS ABOUND. Shockingly, false fathers are proliferating now more than at any time in history. The *false* is appearing *real* to more and more men and therefore to a vastly increasing number of our young.

When the *false* becomes *real* in our minds and hearts, deception has overwhelmed and replaced truth and reality. The dangers lurking in such deception defy discipleship and are dangerously defining a very unexpected and unpleasant destiny for our children and grandchildren. Of this deadly spiritual sleight of hand, we have been specifically forewarned.

THE FATHER'S FOREWARNING

A true and genuine father will forewarn his children of the dangers lurking around them that may not be apparent or appreciated by their youthful eyes, minds and hearts. He will also be alert to warnings that may not be for youthful ears but rather for those who, at least to all appearances by virtue of age, should be able to detect the reality of such warnings, and discern their implications for his family . . . or his congregation.

A true and genuine father will forewarn his children.

Our heavenly Father has, as a genuine father, done just that. His warnings are woven throughout the Bible so that fathers may be prepared to protect their families. In surprising truth, most of the Father's warnings, while applying to all time, apply with immensely greater import to our time . . . this very season of history in which you and I live. That understanding should grip every father's heart, driving us with provoking gratitude to prepare our sons and daughters to embrace the *real* and reject the *false*.

The lamentable problem lies in the fact that so many *Christian* fathers have themselves become so enveloped with the false that the real appears of little genuine significance. In effect, we become like the blind leading the blind. And that is of little comfort when the eternal precipice lies straight ahead. Might many be unwittingly leading their children into the waiting arms of the ultimate *false father*, who seeks but for to steal, kill and destroy (John 10:10)?

The *false father* is Satan, the *deceiver*. It may be shocking, but Jesus described the trusted religious leaders of His day (seen as the spiritual fathers) as being "of your father the devil," who is "a liar, and the father of it" (John 8:44). Jesus, therefore, said that these purported and trusted spiritual *fathers* were "blind leaders of the blind" (Matt. 15:14). They were seen and trusted as *fathers*, but, from the Father's viewpoint, they were more deceived than those they sought to disciple. And that is a significant part of our problem today, on the near edge of history's final hour.

The apostle Peter warned of the "pernicious ways" of false fathers with profound gravity (1 Peter 2:1–3). False teachers and false prophets are nothing more than false fathers who lead many unsuspecting spiritual children astray. John also spoke of these counterfeits, warning, "Little children, it is the last time [last days] . . . Even now there are many antichrists; whereby we know that it is the last time" (1 John 2:18). Paul, not to be outdone in his warning, declared, "But evil men and seducers shall wax worse and worse, deceiving and being deceived" (2 Tim. 3:13). He spoke of those who appeared to be trusted fathers within the body of Christ.

How extensively will deception by false fathers define our times in these latter days of what we know as the end-times?

How extensively will deception by false fathers define our times in these latter days of what we know as the *end*-times?

Jesus minced no words, warning that "many false prophets shall rise, and shall deceive many." The reason for this is that "iniquity shall abound, and the love of many shall wax cold," not only in the culture but especially in the church. "Many shall come in my name . . . and shall deceive many" (Matt. 24: 1–12, 5). Just how greatly will we, and our children, be enveloped and driven by the overwhelming deception of false fathers? "If it were possible," lamented Jesus, "they shall deceive the very elect [remnant of those *claiming* to be believers]" (Matt. 24:24).

TO BE FOREWARNED IS TO BE FOREARMED

As we have seen, there is an ultimate "false father." It is his sole goal to turn all fathers in this ultimate moment of human history against the Father of our Lord, Jesus Christ, "of whom the whole family in heaven and earth is named" (Eph. 3:14-15). He must accomplish, and is actually accomplishing, his goal through deceit and seduction. Since no man is ever truly seduced or deceived against his will, how do we as fathers resist Satan's pernicious ploys, securing a pure and holy pathway for our sons and daughters?

The apostle Peter gives us some very clear truths to which we can cling to keep us from collapsing into the arms of false fathers—or becoming false fathers ourselves. These truths enable us and our children to "escape the corruption that is in the world" (2 Peter 4:4). In 2 Peter 1, this apostle, once vacillating but now victorious, taught us these principles. Let's take a look.

1. All things that pertain both to life and to godliness HAVE ALREADY BEEN GIVEN to us. We simply must embrace them fully and practice them faithfully (v. 3).

2. God's promises enable us, as earthly fathers, to partake of the Father's own nature, when embraced fully and practiced faithfully (v. 4). When the Father's nature is displayed in and through our nature, our children will see it, exchanging perceived hypocrisy for holiness.

3. By the Father's promises, we are enabled as fathers to "escape the corruption that is in the world" that propels us to conform to the will and ways of the false father, the Father's archenemy—and your enemy (vv. 3, 4).

Having established this foundational vision and viewpoint, we are then enjoined to extraordinary attitude-and-action-specific behavior that defies the destructive ways of the false father. These very specific requirements determine whether we fail or faithfully succeed in transmitting a godly legacy. Dare we take a look? Effectuating these consistently will require a level of diligence seldom found among professing Christian men today (v. 5).

1. ADD TO YOUR PROFESSED FAITH, *VIRTUE*. This may seem simple, but when we consider that virtue, like truth, has fallen on very hard times over the last two generations, it may well be that we no longer even comprehend the meaning of *virtue*. "Liberty and Virtue" once embellished the banners of America, but no longer. We have convinced ourselves that liberty can be claimed despite virtue having been lost.

Just a generation ago, *Forbes*, the premier business magazine of America, devoted its entire seventy-fifth anniversary edition to exploring the profound effect of loss of virtue in America and how, if possible, to recover it. Statistics for the past generation reveal a profound disconnect between our alleged profession of Christian faith and the practical ways in which we live our lives. Do we really imagine . . . with a straight face . . . that our children and grandchildren do not see this hypocritical disconnect, and then embrace it for themselves as somehow defining the way things should be done as "people of faith"?

Perhaps the closest biblical word giving full meaning to *virtue* is the word *righteousness*. Righteousness, distilled, means "right-ways-ness" from the Father's viewpoint as revealed, with particularity, in His Word. So, where do we, as fathers—and as those who claim to be *spiritual* fathers—stand with regard to *righteousness*?

So, where do we, as fathers—and as those who claim to be spiritual fathers—stand with regard to righteousness?

Perhaps this brief story will drive home the likely answers. It is unforgettable to me. It was about ten years ago. As I was driving to a monthly pastors' breakfast for the *birth city* of America, I asked the Father why, after so many years of praying for revival, both in our city and across the land, we had really seen no honest fruit. Father's answer was immediate and specific: "My pastors are not preaching righteousness." The words were both persuasive and profound. They could not be dismissed.

When I arrived at our meeting, we were socializing over coffee before breakfast. A local pastor of a very large and respected evangelical church with historical roots in the holiness movement came up to me. I shared briefly my short conversation with the Father. This pastor's response is indelibly impressed upon my spiritual memory and defines our choice for either horror or hope in the future of our homes.

Before I reveal his response, I must encourage you to fasten your faith seatbelt so as to prevent spiritual whiplash. Are you ready? This highly touted evangelical pastor hung his head and breathed these words . . . "I'm not sure I even know how to preach righteousness." That, brethren, is the plague defining a progressively virtueless nation and church in which we endeavor to *disciple* our sons and daughters.

The glory has departed from both family and nation as we seek to present a virtueless gospel in a country and world demanding *authenticity*. As *Time* so aptly described the situation, we are living in and defining a *fake-real* world of *synthetic authenticity*.[1]

We are living in and defining a fake-real world of synthetic authenticity.

This may well be our greatest problem in leaving a godly legacy that will truly last. Repentance alone provides hope, since we are so clearly warned: "Righteousness [alone] exalteth a nation: but sin is a reproach to any people" (Prov. 14:34). Virtue must be restored, not only as a principle but in practice, if we even hope to have victory in this warfare with the false father.

2. TO *VIRTUE* WE MUST ADD *KNOWLEDGE* (2 Peter 1:5). But of what *knowledge* does Peter speak? He tells us in verse 2. It is the knowledge *of* God, not knowledge *about* God. In this Information Age, it is easy to confuse or conflate the two, and we usually do to our peril.

Our lives as men and fathers are to reflect, insofar as humanly possible, the divine nature of the Father that we might be *partakers* of His very nature (v. 4). When we partake of the Father's nature, our children are far more likely to *partake* of the Father's nature by seeing it borne out in both spirit and truth. Hearts will then turn, both to us and to the Father. This is the *turning* of the hearts of which the prophet Malachi has spoken (Mal. 4:5–6).

3. TO THE *KNOWLEDGE* OF GOD WE MUST ADD *TEMPERANCE* (2 Peter 1:6). Some have translated this as *self-control*. If we, as self-professing *Christian* fathers, cannot or will not control ourselves to obey the Father, how in this world can we expect our children and grandchildren to obey us respectfully? Just asking . . .

4. TO *TEMPERANCE*, OR SELF-CONTROL, WE MUST ADD *PATIENCE*. Patience is perhaps the most difficult and oft-repeated lesson we must learn and live. While varying personalities may appear to "be patient" more than others, we all are confronted with the need for fatherly patience.

James, Jesus' brother, well understood the power and purpose of patience. He encouraged, "Let patience have her perfect work, that ye may be perfect, wanting [or lacking] nothing" (James 1:4). Yet it is that which we loathe—the "trying of our faith"—that produces patience (v. 3).

Here comes the inevitable rhetorical question again. How can we fathers expect our sons and daughters to persevere through trials and temptations when they do not see Dad do so, perfected through patience? This pattern of fatherly persistence through patience so as to embrace the promises that open to us and our children the "divine nature" is what protects both them . . . and us . . . from the seduction of the false father.

How can we fathers expect our sons and daughters to persevere through trials and temptations when they do not see Dad do so through patience?

---

5. TO EVER-PERFECTING *PATIENCE* WE ARE TO ADD *GODLINESS* (2 Peter 1:6). Godliness does not materialize merely through a confession of faith but rather through faithful embracing of the promises that increasingly invest the divine nature in our lives. That is why, as fathers, we are to "be doers of the Word, and not hearers only, deceiving our own selves" (James 1:22).

When we convince ourselves that a mere confession of faith, without godly living, will change the hearts of our children, we deceive not only ourselves but them as well. If indeed virtue and righteousness have fallen on hard times, it should be immediately apparent that godliness is in profoundly short supply as well.

When we convince ourselves that a mere confession of faith, without godly living, will change the hearts of our children, we deceive not only ourselves but them as well.

Godliness is having attitudes and actions that depict in our own lives the divine nature of the Father. Where do we, where do you, stand, by the measure of the Father's plumb line?

6. BROTHERLY *KINDNESS* MUST EMBELLISH *GODLINESS* (2 Peter 1:7). I sorely wish we did not have to discuss this. Please try to be patient. With grief we must address a grievous problem that persistently compromises our testimony.

How easy it is, in the warmth of a worship experience, to be transported into the very heavenlies, only to crash to an ignominious splattering of our self-professed purported faith on the earthly tarmac of fatherly disgrace.

Such is the painful picture of both natural and *spiritual* fathers whose reputations, in an instant, are destroyed or seriously impaired by a lack of brotherly love. And our children, in horror, witness the debacle and determine to distance themselves from *the faith* or, conversely, to become just like Dad . . . or the pastor. Legacy is on the line! And we have all been there. Wow! Time to take a breath!

Feelings are not faith; neither is biblical love defined by our feelings. Such love is better defined practically as brotherly kindness. We are kind because we share in the divine nature, and then, it is the goodness and kindness of God the Father that leads us to repentance when we become shockingly aware of our unkindness (Rom. 2:4). We are kind because all are made in the image of the Father.

What, then, should we make of it . . . or our children—when we, in hot pursuit of *spiritual truth* in the name of our particular theological persuasion, engage in verbal fisticuffs, become red in the face, and breach any divine protocol of spirit? Does not our pride destroy desire for brotherly kindness, making a mockery of our professed love for the Father? Should we not be more sensitive to the Father's viewpoint as He patiently puts up with all of us who so persistently . . . and ineptly . . . live out our alleged faith?

Indeed! There is a place for truth, but should we not be more prone to remember that it is the Father's truth, not ours? Can we be truth lovers and truth protectors without "burning our brethren at the stake" of self-righteousness, as did many of even our more famous forebears, supposed *fathers* of the faith?

Over forty years of ministry, first as a trial attorney whose clients came primarily from the Body of Christ, then as a pastor and broadcaster, I must report that many of the most wicked displays of unkindness have been perpetrated in the alleged pursuit of biblical truth. And by far the worst offenders are those who have embraced humanly defined theological constructs and frameworks that are presented as the fullness of gospel truth. Man moves into these systems and lamentably, would rather die on the hill of their particular theological culture than on the hill of Christ under the cross.

Only the Father's truth will ultimately stand and unite true followers and fathers in Christ. As prayed Jesus, "Sanctify them [set them apart] through thy truth; thy word is truth" (John

17:17). We are not the Father but rather sons, who in humility are seeking to follow the Father revealed in His Son, who is "full of grace and truth." Let us be lovers of truth AND lovers of the brethren.

And finally in this regard . . . the subject of *apologetics* comes to mind. No, we need not make an apology for seeking to, as it is written "be ready always to give an answer to every man that asketh you a reason for the hope that is in you with meekness and fear" (1 Peter 3:15). The problem is not with "the reason for the hope." The real problem is with the one who purports to *reason*. It is one thing to *reason*, yet quite another to confront and combat, thinking that the greater vigor will render me the victor as "king of the mountain," enabling me to leave the arena with pride.

When our children, as our spiritual progeny, observe such behavior that devolves often into a debacle, or when they hear us (whether in our homes or congregations) report of such events, are they seeing brotherly kindness exemplified, or rather a bawdy display of that which defames the name of the Father and His Son? Perhaps, to help us in dealing with the seduction of the false father that draws us into such fleshly pursuits, it might be helpful to remember the words of a famous bard: "A man convinced against his will is of the same opinion still." We do not, gentlemen, wish to "give place to the devil," do we?

7. TO BROTHERLY *KINDNESS* WE MUST ADD *CHARITY* (2 Peter 1:7). Brotherly kindness is primarily an attitude. Charity is an action that flows from genuine Fatherly love and kindness.

Imagine the import to the watchful eyes of those we hope to disciple for a godly destiny when they see Dad give, not reluctantly but cheerfully, as a *Kingdom conduit* of the Father's heart and blessing. Just think of your child's perception of the Father when he or she witnesses the earthly father, who is so trusted, giving joyously rather than grudgingly when needs are presented or become apparent.

Just think of your child's perception of the Father when he or she witnesses the earthly father.

The attitude and the action become wedded to display the glory and grace of the Father on this seemingly selfish and scorched-earth plane.

HOW TO "NEVER FALL"

Opportunity and hope lie straight ahead! That is when we consider the big little word *if*. Dads . . . grandfathers . . . pastors . . . are you ready? Are you absolutely sure? Then here is the apostle Peter's conclusion of the matter.

> For *if* these things be in you, and abound, they make you that ye shall neither be barren nor unfruitful in the knowledge *of* [not about] our Lord Jesus Christ (2 Peter 1:8).

Unfortunately, there is always a *but*. And the *buts* are as important as the *ifs*.

> *But* he that lacketh these things is blind, and cannot see afar

off [can't see the legacy down the road], and hath forgotten that he was purged from his old sins (v. 9).

Here, then, is Peter's conclusion and benediction, which gives us eternal hope if we heed the divinely ordained pattern for fathering.

Wherefore the rather, brethren, give diligence to make your calling [as a father] and election sure: for *if* ye do these things, ye shall never fall (v. 10).

Flee the false father at every juncture. Submit to the Father and His ways at every intersection. Then resist the devil. If we, as fathers, try to resist the devil without first and continuously submitting to God the Father, our children will most likely languish in the arms of the false father, and our legacy will be lost. Do not let that happen. If we are concerned about a legacy, the future is NOW. So...give diligence!

PROBING OUR HEARTS

1. How would you describe a *false father*?

2. Are there any characteristics about your own life that might tend to make you somewhat of a *false father*?

3. How are you preparing your children or grandchildren to identify the *false* in a *fake-real* world?

4. Why is *righteousness* the centerpiece of discerning between the false and the real?

5. Of all the *spiritual characteristics* described in 2 Peter 1, as specifically discussed in this chapter, are there any in which you find your own life weak, perhaps compromising your legacy as a father?

17

SHOW-AND-TELL TIME

It's time we had a national conversation about the important role of fatherhood and how important It is that we get fatherly examples and role models.

—CONGRESSMAN BILL JOHNSON, AUTHOR OF *RAISING FATHERS*

A FATHER'S GREAT COMMISSION is to make disciples. Yet it is painfully apparent that many fathers—yes, even pastors and spiritual leaders—are more dedicated to saving the world than to discipling their own children and grandchildren. It is a travesty of monumental and eternal proportions, and we are paying the profound cultural consequences. So . . . what must we do?

COMMANDED TO DISCIPLE
All who truly follow Jesus as Lord are commanded by the Father to make disciples, modeled after and "conformed to the image

of His Son," Yeshua Messiah, that He might be "the firstborn of *many* brethren" (Rom. 8:29). The Father has deputized us to be doers of that holy calling so that Christ's kingdom may come and the Father's will be done on earth as it is in heaven (Matt. 6:10).

There is no greater calling than to fulfill this *Great Commission*, yet the commission itself is almost always misinterpreted and misunderstood, with the emphasis falsely placed on sowing spiritual sperm rather than raising up godly sons and daughters. Furthermore, the marketed focus of the Great Commission, so as to raise funds for *ministry* and *missionary* endeavors, shifts our attention, with seemingly good intentions, away from the foundational focus of discipling sons, daughters and grandchildren in our families. This familiar and persistent failure over generations has led to the progressive deterioration of the culture—indeed, of the church itself—as revealed by nearly all statistics for the present generation as well as the generation past. Should it come as a surprise, then, that "all of the foundations of the earth are out of course" (Ps. 82:5)?

What, then, is the Great Commission? Is it to birth spiritual babies, many who die in infancy due to lack of care, or is it not rather, in first and primary substance, to raise up sons, daughters, and grandchildren to spiritual maturity as foundational to reaching the world for Christ?

Discipling is not a program to be institutionally devised but a life to be inspirationally lived

---

Discipling is not a program to be institutionally devised but a life to be inspirationally and intentionally lived to both declare the Word and display the Father, just as Jesus did. And Jesus made clear the central call of the Great Commission. It is "teaching [our families] to observe [obey] all things whatsoever I have commanded you" (Matt. 28:20). Evangelism, as the Scriptures make clear, is only a beginning step, not the primary goal or purpose of discipleship. The harder and perhaps holier part of that work is the daily declaration and display of the Father's kingdom household in our own households and localized relationships where we have influence.

Perhaps we should really probe deeply into our heart motivation that leads us to focus primarily into "going into all the world" while passively avoiding the more profound yet less public task of persistent discipleship in our own homes. Lamentably, for those seeking public or denominational recognition and fund-raising markers, a father's faithful discipleship at home carries little appreciated weight because his fruit cannot be immediately measured for marketing.

It is not that evangelism as commonly practiced should not be practiced, but rather that it should be given its proper place as merely ushering in spiritual birth as opposed to being seen as fulfilling the Great Commission, which demands the hard and almost unmarketable labor of lifelong discipleship required of all fathers, whether natural or spiritual. As Jesus noted on another issue, "[This] ought ye to have done, and not to leave the other undone" (Matt. 23:23).

If the hearts of the fathers are to be truly turned to the children, there must be a course correction in ministry thinking and practice.

At first blush, this may seem offensive because evangelism, as commonly understood (spiritual baby making through *new birth*), has been persistently elevated to an unbiblical or distorted role in the greater calling and declared purpose of the Great Commission. Yet if the hearts of the fathers are to be truly turned in a fully biblical way to the children, there must be a course correction in ministry thinking and practice. How many pastors, parachurch ministers, evangelists and missionaries have left their own sons and daughters to languish un-discipled in the spiritual dust in pursuit of "saving the lost," leaving angry, abandoned, and even apostate children to be discipled by a godless culture? A father's heart will largely determine his spiritual heritage. For what shall it profit a man if he undertakes to save the whole world yet loses the soul of his family (see Matt. 16:26)?

THE HEART OF DISCIPLESHIP

There are three kinds of *knowledge*: head knowledge, heart knowledge and experiential knowledge. Similarly, there are three aspects to true discipleship: information, transformation and application. Remember: information without transformation leads to spiritual frustration, stagnation and even termination. The bridge between information and transformation is application. Application is the

"Word" being "made flesh," resulting in behavior and attitudes that conform increasingly to what we *say* we believe.

This understanding cannot be overemphasized for fathers, whether natural or spiritual. Yet for the majority of fathers, whether natural or *spiritual*, some form of catechism or presenting mere Bible information and facts is deemed to satisfy the demand for discipleship. Yet information and religious facts neither give life to a father's discipleship nor breathe life-giving transformation to the children.

So, what does this mean for fathers and grandfathers, or even for those who want to see themselves as spiritual *fathers*? Expressed simply, it means that the centerpiece of the Great Commission is not the *head* but rather the *heart*. Biblical information without continuous and corrective application may inform the head but cannot change the heart. Yet if our own *fatherly* faith consists primarily of biblical information and facts of the faith, we are incapable of true, life-giving discipleship, leaving our children's hearts unchanged.

Biblical information without continuous and corrective application may inform the head but cannot change the heart.

This is why a father's heart must first be captured by Christ, not merely by a cerebral confession of faith but by a complete conversion of both mind and heart leading to clearly observable changes in both attitudes and actions. Only then can the hearts of the children be turned toward their fathers. And this heart transformation is what is profoundly lacking among professing *Christian* men. Therefore, when our children and grandchildren observe our lives, they see not *holiness* but *hypocrisy*. *Discipleship* takes place, not toward advancing faith, but toward distrust, disgust, and cynicism leading increasingly to abandonment of biblical faith.

DISTILLED DISCIPLESHIP

What, then, is discipleship? What is the Father's viewpoint? What was Jesus' understanding, seeing that He said, "I and My Father are one" (John 10:30) and "He that hath seen Me, hath seen the Father" (John 14:9) and "My Father is greater than I" (John 14:28)?

The Father's focus on the Great Commission was exactly this: "teaching them to observe [obey] all things that I have commanded you" (Matt. 28:20). The Father's greatest desire was not confession of faith but conversion or transformation of heart revealed in an ever-increasing life pattern of TRUST and OBEY.

This is the essence and enveloping purpose of a father's life in discipling his children. So we must each ask ourselves . . . "How do I measure up?" What continuing observable and practical evidence reveals an ever-increasing pattern of heart expression in trusting and obeying the Father? What does my wife think? What might others think by observing the attitudes and actions of my children?

Life as a follower of Christ then becomes real . . . almost tangible . . . because truth is displayed not just in what I say or claim to believe, but in how I live. And my heart is turned, in spirit and in truth, toward my sons and daughters, followed responsively by their hearts turning trustingly to me.

It is truly "show-and-tell" time for fathers if we are to prepare our progeny for Christ's coming. Are we up to the call? Are we willing to accept the challenge as a man and "step up to the plate" in holy hope? Time is fleeting faster and faster. Let's seize the moment.

PROBING OUR HEARTS

1. Based on the specific words of Jesus in Matthew 28:20, what is the heart or primary focus of the *Great Commission*?

2. As a Christian father, do you find yourself majoring on *head* knowledge or *heart* knowledge in the training and instruction of your children?

3. How would you define *discipleship* from Jesus' perspective?

4. What observable evidence can you point to showing an ever-increasing pattern of your children's hearts in trusting and obeying the Father?

5. On a scale of 1 to 10, where do you rank as a father in genuine spiritual discipleship (do NOT count church attendance)?

18

DISCIPLING FOR DESTINY

As priest you represent your family to God;
As prophet you represent God to your family.
—DEREK PRINCE, HUSBANDS & FATHERS

THE PREMIER DUTY OF DADS is to disciple their sons and daughters for destiny. All other expectations of fathers, while not diminished in value, are secondary in purpose. Discipleship is the fulcrum over which a father's legacy either succeeds or fails.

BECOMING DADS OF DESTINY
The word *destiny*, while seemingly simple, is actually a bit more elusive in definition than we might think. The reason is that our perception of the nature of destiny, what destiny looks like, and what we desire for it to be depends on the father's viewpoint and values. If a dad embraces the more predominant values

and goods defined by the surrounding culture, the culture itself defines the destiny of his children. The father's life values have set the course. His daily decisions are defining the destiny of the children . . . or grandchildren . . . whether or not he cares to admit it.

We, as fathers, became surrogates for the Heavenly Father in raising up our children.

On the other hand, the Father has defined discipling for destiny quite differently. "Train up a child in the way he should go," we are told (Prov. 22:6). What, then, does it mean to *train*, and who determines *the way he should go*? Training is a form of discipline in a particular direction. The *way a child should go* is to be determined and defined by the Father, who gave the instructions to us. We, as fathers, became surrogates for the Heavenly Father in raising up our children. Our continual inward cry must be that of Jesus, the Son, "Not mine own will, but the will of the Father which hath sent me" (John 5:30; Luke 22:42).

UNDER AUTHORITY

Just as Jesus the Son was under the Father's absolute authority, so are we as dads. But to what extent do we either daily acknowledge that authority or willingly and joyfully submit to it? And how, under heaven, can we ever truly hope to have our children willingly and joyfully submit to our authority on earth when we, in whole or in part, refuse to do the same with our heavenly Father?

This is the fulcrum issue that will determine whether or not we will leave a godly legacy that lasts.

Am I truly a dad or grandfather under authority? Do I agree with the Father's express viewpoint on the issues of life and practice? Do I really believe that I have been delegated the task of discipling my children for destiny in accordance with the Father's will?

This is not merely a matter of cognitive assent to a statement of faith but rather an active pursuit to carry out that which I say I believe. The words *believe, trust* and *faith* must become one in operation if we dads are to carry out our delegated authority with integrity. That requires a profound and provocative lifelong decision that will define the destiny of our young. Regretfully, most professing Christian men today neither understand the gravity of this authority nor embrace it, thus seriously compromising any real legacy that will last.

WHAT IS DISCIPLING?

Christian discipling is quite simply training our sons and daughters in the Word, Will and Ways of the Lord. It includes the Great Commission, "...baptizing them . . . [and] teaching them to observe [obey] all things the Father has commanded" (Matt. 28:19–20).

The call and command to discipleship is a father's greatest responsibility, a nondelegable duty.

The call and command to discipleship is a father's greatest responsibility. Discipleship is a nondelegable duty. Sending or taking our children to church is only one part of that discipling process. The greater part is done at home. Just as home is the heart of the family, so it is the heart and centerpiece of all ongoing discipleship. If genuine and consistent discipleship is not a major part of a father's vision for his family, his family will progressively fail and the father's greatest legacy with his children will be aborted.

The Father has given us clear instructions, in a broad and general way, as to His expectations of fathers serving as His surrogates. We know them, yet find it difficult to remember and do them.

> Thou shalt love the LORD thy God with all thine heart, and with all thy soul, and with all thy might. (Deut. 6:5; see also Deut. 30:6; Matt. 22:37; Mark 12:30; Luke 10:27)

On a scale of 1 to 10, with 10 being the greatest fulfillment of these requirements, where do you stand? If you were to ask each of your children . . . and your spouse . . . where do you think they would honestly rate you, and why? And how about your grandchildren? How would they measure your life as the foundation upon which all discipleship will be, or is being, built? Lastly, think seriously about how your Father would rate your present practices.

> And these words, which I command thee this day, shall be in thine heart:
> And thou shalt teach them diligently unto thy children, and shall talk of them when thou sittest in thine house, and

when thou walkest by the way, and when thou liest down, and when thou risest up. (Deut. 6:6–7)

DISCIPLING BY FAITH

As with all other pursuits in the Christian life, discipling must be done by faith as a clear evidence of what I truly believe and of the great trust I have in the Father to fulfill His purposes as I faithfully and diligently disciple my children. This must be my confidence.

Cast not away therefore your confidence, which hath great recompense of reward.

For ye have need of patience that, after ye have done the will of God, ye might receive the promise. (Heb. 10:35–36)

It is faith in the Father's calling and promises that will enable me to persevere, despite challenges and occasional discouragement. Remember: "the just shall live by faith" . . . not by feelings.

Discipling is a daily pursuit. Our children are continually taking their cues from Dad's attitudes, actions, words and perceived values. Am I arrogant or humble? Am I caring or self-centered? Am I peaceable or angry? Am I diligent or slothful? True faith inevitably reveals itself in the consistency of what I purport to believe and how I actually live.

HOW TO DISCIPLE WITH DILIGENCE

To disciple with diligence is to see the task of discipleship training as ongoing, day after day, season after season, year after year. It becomes a living, breathing part of who I am. Once I catch the vision, it increasingly defines my way of thinking so that discipleship becomes natural and not forced.

Yes, there will be resistance from time to time, but as a father and head of my home, I will not be deterred because I am obeying the Father's will for my family.

For starters, I will . . .

- Pray daily with my wife and family

- Prepare their hearts daily with meaningful passages of Scripture

- Propose activities that will aid in teaching biblical truths

- Promote serving and hospitality

- Provide time for relaxed biblical application and conversation

- Practice regular family worship, even on vacation

PRECIOUS MEMORIES

Many of the most precious memories of my life are related to discipleship. I would like to share a few of them with you, for these memories linger not only in my mind but also in the memories of my daughters and grandchildren. These then become the mortar cementing the building blocks of a lasting legacy.

MEAL TIME

For an understandably busy dad, businessman and lawyer, the evening hours were precious and reserved times for the family, including our mealtime together, always around the table. So significant were those times that my wife would insist on delaying, when necessary, the mealtime so that we could all be together. Just as an aside . . . many of Jesus' most important discipling moments, both with His own disciples and with others, involved breaking bread with them, imparting spiritual truth in relational ways amid the otherwise mundane activities of life . . . and there was no TV or cell phone to distract.

Gracing the wall beside our family table were six beautiful plaques, one for my wife and me and one for each of our daughters. On each plaque was highlighted the person's name and meaning of the name, with a supporting biblical reference. The sixth plaque, designed much like the others, contained the words from Jeremiah 29:11: "For I know the thoughts that I think toward you, saith the LORD, thoughts of peace and not of evil, to give you an expected end." This wall thus set the spirit governing both our meals and other relational moments, to which I made frequent reference so that its implications would be deeply ingrained. So great, in fact, was this ingrained, the desire for which was embraced, that one of our daughters chose to duplicate this wall for her own family . . . so the legacy lasts . . . or at least lingers to the next generation.

Our meal times were opportunities for the joys and sorrows of the day to be spilled out, either spontaneously or prodded. As head of the home, I was able to discern those areas in which each child might need fatherly guidance as revealed in and through the Father's Word, whether for encouragement, adding necessary aspects to their faith, or for correction in righteousness. My wife did not allow backbiting, belittling and banal gossip to besmirch the spirit of these precious times.

In retrospect, the great value of these carefully preserved meal times was not so much in the momentous effect of any singular experience. Rather, it was the aggregate of a practice perceived dear over years that has prevailed for discipleship impact . . . as it is written, "precept upon precept; line upon line, . . . here a little, and there a little" (Isa. 28:10).

BED TIMES

Bed times were beloved times . . . mostly. Mom had the guidance of the kids by day, and dad usually by night, with comparatively few exceptions.

Putting our daughters to bed at night was a paternal priority that mom supported enthusiastically.

Putting our daughters to bed at night and setting the stage was a paternal priority that mom supported enthusiastically. But these were not "Now I lay me down to sleep . . ." times. They demanded of dad personal discipline drawn from personal desire to personally disciple these precious daughters. And that does not come easily when a father's day has been intensely invested in solving other people's or families' conflicts.

So memorable were these bedtime moments over months and years that our daughters, though now shepherding grown and growing families, will never forget them. And where there is no forgetting that which has been fatherly invested, there remains a waiting legacy when fertilized in the next generation.

Where there is no forgetting that which has been fatherly invested, there remains a waiting legacy.

Of what, then, did these bedtimes consist? Where did these memorable times take place, and for how long? And why might they be so memorable?

These were profound *with you* times. I wanted my daughters to understand deeply and daily that their father desired to be *with them* so that they might, over time, similarly understand that the Father desires to be *with* us and that we should seek His presence daily. So these moments were never rushed, nor were they mere ritual. Rather, they established the *right* for relational discipleship, imparting the Father's living truths through a sense of togetherness that was deeply felt.

Every bedtime experience was framed around the Father's Word. As the girls, over time, saw and heard their father embrace the Father's Word, will and ways, they also began to internalize those same passions and purposes. Yet these times were seldom boring. Rather, the manner in which I related the biblical stories breathed life into what otherwise may have been perceived as mere *stories*. Sometimes I would read them, but most often told them with a life-giving passion from the heart that drove an otherwise seemingly mundane message deep into the girls' memories.

Often, so as to increase memorability, I would dramatize the story (or a certain portion of it) so that it was driven indelibly into their spiritual memory. And to this day, the girls remember these memory reinforcements, knowing that I may, on occasion, repeat them even in their grown years, for passing on to their children, thus the legacy is given continuing life.

Yet no biblical story or account was ever presented without specific purpose, for the Bible is not a storybook of fascinating fables but rather a series of accounts of the ways the Father works, why God has done or responded as He has over history, and how we today should take heed, applying these principles, purposes and practices in our own lives, defining the ways in which we both think and act. In this way, these times were both loaded with truth and prepared for life transformation.

But there is a further aspect of these bedtimes during the girls' childhood that, I believe, helped to bind us together and with the Father as we shared the Father's Word. And that is the power of *touch*. As I would gather the girls closely together under my *wings*, they could better feel the foundations of a real faith. As they could tangibly experience the touch of their earthly father's arms, so they might internalize more deeply the desire of the Father to touch their lives in a transformative reality that would otherwise be difficult to communicate.

Yet to enable all this to happen, over months and years, I must admit it required not only desire, but discipline and persistence. I could not allow a day's weariness or tiredness to distract or deter from such a holy endeavor. Each evening presented a decision as to whether or not I would be a faithful dad and surrogate for my Father. Time becomes the true test of trust and testimony.

SEIZING TEACHABLE MOMENTS

The Father instructs us as His surrogates, to speak of his Word *when we walk by the way, when we rise up and when we lie down* (Deut. 6:7). If we have eyes to see, ears to hear and hearts to understand, we will increasingly see the vast opportunities to communicate and apply spiritual truth throughout most of our ongoing experiences with our families. Life and discipleship then take on all new meaning, joy and purpose. This has become a way of life that both my children and grandchildren well know. It is not set aside time for some didactic teaching but real, in-the-trenches truth that makes discipleship become truly a way of life.

These teachable moments can occur almost any time and under almost any circumstances. If not seen and seized, the opportunity is lost. Working in the yard, experiencing the weather, hiking a trail, climbing rocks, engaging in a project . . . virtually anything can give rise to a moment that transforms the boring or banal into a blessing.

One such unforgettable moment occurred at ten thousand feet elevation in the Yosemite high country when our firstborn was barely a toddler. Our tent was set up after a goodly hike, but I could not sleep. And so I crawled out of my bag, put on my down jacket, grabbed Nicole, and took her out on a rock, where I wrapped her in my arms, talking both to her and to the Father. With stars glistening, in the stillness of God's glory being displayed overhead, Nicole could experience the warmth not only of her father's presence but also that of the Father as we conversed together, heart to heart. The glory of that moment, perhaps an hour, cannot be adequately grasped by one who had not experienced it. Unforgettable!

Teachable moments begin in infancy.

Teachable moments begin in infancy. I had such a heart for the Father that I wanted my girls to know and sense that early on. I spoke of Him often, usually when tenderly touching them, declaring His heart for them and His purposes and promises made available through His Son, Jesus. And they could only listen.

In particular, when our oldest was less than a year old, I would frequently take her in my fatherly arms, wrap her warmly, and carry her closely in the evening for a walk with the Father. I spoke to Him about her and His plan and purposes. I spoke to her, seeking to bathe her mind in the mind of Christ, so that when she could speak, she might speak His Word for herself.

What is the measure of such moments? Only time will tell. But I am convinced now, as then, that any legacy that will last begins today.

Regretfully, I must confess that few, if any, of the principles and practices shared herein were experienced by my growing up in a pastor's home. Most such experiences came through my mother. In fairness, however, fathers of past generations worked a standard six-day week, and life was generally harder. In addition, sternness tended to be predominant, with tenderness given little value. The fullness of genuine manhood is now mandated if we hope to leave a legacy that will last.

PROBING OUR HEARTS

1. What is the premier duty of dads from the Father's viewpoint?

2. Do you actually see yourself as the Father's surrogate in raising and discipling your children and grandchildren? If not, how might that make a difference?

3. As a follower of Christ, do you consider yourself to be under the Father's absolute authority, as Jesus did? Does your life reveal that submission to the Father's will as did Jesus'?

4. On a scale of 1 to 10, where do you think your wife would rate your spiritual discipleship of your children?

5. Based upon your current and recent past spiritual discipleship of your children, what do you think (not hopefully, but realistically) will be your spiritual legacy?

6. What steps, if any, are you convicted to change in order to leave a spiritual legacy that will last?

19

SEVEN FATHERLY SECRETS

*The words that a father speaks to his children in the privacy of home . . .
are clearly heard at the end by posterity.*

—JEAN PAUL RICHTER

GLUE BONDS THE BROKEN TOGETHER. And relationships between fathers and children are often bruised and broken. Such bruising and brokenness can be the result of fatherly failures, or it can be the result of other experiences or thinking of our children that may tend to either frustrate or seemingly prevent the kind of hope-filled relationship in which a godly legacy can grow.

Here we want to deliver hope through seven fatherly secrets that can provide the relational *glue* needed so that our desired legacy has the needed relational environment to not only grow but become joyful and fulfilling in the journey. These seven *secrets*, each distilled into a single key word, may seem simple, but together they are extraordinarily powerful—like Gorilla Glue. They collectively play together like instruments in a concert.

TIME. Time is the quintessential ingredient for all meaningful and satisfying relationship. And it is the same for every father. The hours of day and evening are equal for every dad. How that time is used or allocated among the demands and decisions of our lives often determines or sets the course of destiny both for ourselves and for our families.

All things considered, time is ultimately our most valuable commodity. We spend money to *save* time. But for what purpose have we *saved* it? Have we saved it for personal or selfish purposes, or have we saved it to invest in the people in our spheres of influence, beginning with our wives and children? And how have we balanced that investment between those things that have ultimate or eternal value as compared with those things framed by cultural *mandates* and fleshly *desires* promising only temporal satisfaction? Our decisions today, promising destiny tomorrow, are all framed by time.

TOGETHER. Time does not stand alone, isolated from that which we do with it. Many a father, yes even Christian fathers, co-opt the majority of their *free* time for themselves, having little or no vision for the time value of togetherness. And so precious hours are persistently wasted in pursuits that have no lasting or even present real value.

Precious hours are persistently wasted in pursuits that have no lasting or even present real value.

Multiplied hours passively watching TV, pressing into the latest video games, provoked to near addiction by the clarion call of computers and cell phones, not to mention clandestine peering into porn, have captured the minds and, yes, hearts of a majority of men who otherwise, in public, would declare their desire for a godly legacy. Yet their daily practices in the use of their time tells a very different story.

Time spent together with our wives and children is not defined by whether we are at home, whether we are in the same room, or whether we seem to be engaged even in the same activity, such as sports. Time genuinely *together* requires that state of mind and heart that clearly contributes to a sense of oneness. True togetherness is almost tangible in the taste that it leaves, both when we are together and when we are apart. It has a profound effect on the memory and provides the necessary relational womb for fatherly ministry.

It is the profound sense of presence that lubricates a father's life legacy.

It is the profound sense of *presence* that lubricates a father's life legacy. As we so frequently sing of our Father, "O, the glory of Your presence . . . !" And it is because of the Father's profound presence for which we yearn that "we Your temple give You reverence."

TALKING. Togetherness demands life-giving communication. Without the perception of such life-giving communication, the very concept of togetherness has a very hollow ring. It becomes an illusion, like clouds without rain—a promise that remains painfully unfulfilled.

Our wives, I have learned over fifty years, absolutely crave not only our time together, but that *togetherness* be fulfilled in the manner in which we invest our time in relational conversation. The same is true with our children. While a father must necessarily be stern at times when correction is needed, Dad must also be perceived as *special* in his gentleness toward both sons and daughters. Perception is our children's reality.

Is that not why, as the Father's children, we have so loved that hymn of yesteryear . . . "And He walks with me, and He talks with me . . ."? How then do we respond? "And He tells me I am His own. And the joy we share, as we tarry there, none other has ever known." Need more be said?

THINKING. Have you noticed that women tend to *think out loud* while men tend to think internally, followed by speaking externally to the facts? In one sense it could be actually said that, "Well, that just shows how men and women are different." And that would be true, at least in part. Women tend to *think out loud* primarily because their thoughts are more emotionally engaged than are men's thoughts. For us men, it is "Just the facts, ma'am!"

So . . . men, let's think about how we think and how we speak. There is hope for our tied tongues that find it so difficult to think out loud relationally. The heart of the matter is not only male habits but our hearts. We seriously do not want to be feminized, yet we want to be more effective at speaking *family*, spelled R-E-L-A-T-I-O-N-S-H-I-P. Confidentially, it took me more than thirty years to finally figure it out with my wife, yet

I was able early on to engage in this manner with my daughters.

A man's heart must supersede the mere informational dictate of his mind so that he can speak relationally. That requires the loving sacrifice of more time together talking. The dedication of a father's time to a quality of togetherness allows not only for informational talking but for transformational thinking together. The hearts of both children and dad then become strangely warmed, as does a wife's heart.

Finally, consider this. Our Father made plain the importance of such thinking by declaring "I know the thoughts that I think toward you . . . thoughts of peace and not of evil, to give unto you an expected end"—a hope and a future (Jer. 29:11). Do your children truly know the innermost fatherly thoughts that you internally think toward them? Are they comforted in the belief that your very thoughts promise a hope and a future?

THANKING. There is a quality of thinking that supersedes all others. It is called *gratitude*. Gratitude greases relationship like nothing else.

The Father has taught us, "In everything give thanks: for this is the will of God . . . concerning you" (1 Thess. 5:18). Many a father's failure with his own family can be traced to a lack of gratitude toward his heavenly Father. If I am not truly grateful to God as Father, how can I expect my sons and daughters to be grateful to me?

Many a father's failure with his own family can be traced to a lack of gratitude toward his heavenly Father.

There is great power in gratitude. It is the attitude in which genuine relationship can truly grow. Do your children know how grateful you are for them? How about your wife?

Gratitude is not just a general feeling but must be revealed in specificity and given voice by earnest words that convey the depth of heart connection. But gratitude is not flattery. Flattery is faithless and manipulative. It is insincere and lays a snare for all who hear it. It destroys trust that alone opens the gateway to our proclaiming gospel truth.

TENDERLY. Men often shrink or recoil at the words *tender* and *tenderly* because they seem to convey the aura of the feminine. But there is a masculine tenderness and a feminine tenderness. Together, they make up the "tenderness coin" that is essential in our homes.

Our Father is both firm as a father but tender in His mercies toward us as His children. To understand this we might recall one of the most moving *invitational* hymns of all time: "Softly and tenderly Jesus is calling . . ." These words have touched and drawn the hearts of both men and women into the Father's household. But how is that tenderness expressed? It must be communicated both in attitude and action . . . including words.

TOUCHING. Here is the final secret completing the glue that binds a father's heart with the Father's heart, setting the stage for a godly destiny.

A father's touch is foundational to trust and the communication of truth. When my daughters were young, as we gathered for fatherly bedtime ministry, it was a "hands on" time together. As they felt the warm embrace of their father's arms as I related the Father's truth, they were then able to internalize both their heavenly Father's and earthly father's care. As they have grown through the years and even through married adulthood, that touch is still felt in appropriate ways.

The same is true with grandchildren, whether boy or girl, and whether young or grown. Touch binds the depth of a grandfather's heart into the deepest recesses of the grand kids. And thus they feel the Father's love and often forgiveness.

There is joy unspeakable in a godly father's touch.

There is joy unspeakable in a godly father's touch. Perhaps this is why the Gaither song "He Touched Me" has gained such meaningful traction in the hearts of both men and women, the Father's sons and daughters. The lyrics linger in our spiritual memory:

He touched me . . . O, He touched me

And O, the joy that floods my soul

Something happened, and now I know

He touched me and made me whole

PROBING OUR HEARTS

1. Which one, if any, of the *seven fatherly secrets*, do you think is your strongest suit? Which, if any, is your weakest point?

2. As you look back on your own life growing up, where do you sense your father was weakest . . . and strongest . . . and how have those strengths and weaknesses affected you? Are you passing these same problems down to your own children?

3. On a scale of 1 to 10, where do you think your children would rank you on each of these *seven fatherly secrets*?

4. On a scale of 1 to 10, where do you think your wife would rank you on each of these *seven fatherly secrets*?

5. Have you considered that the focus and time devoted to carrying out these fatherly "secrets" daily is not time and energy wasted, but rather time and energy invested? What difference might such adjusted viewpoint make?

20

FATHERING IN FEARFUL TIMES

We must accept finite disappointment, but we must never lose infinite hope.

—MARTIN LUTHER KING JR.

INCREASING FEAR WILL DEFINE OUR TIMES. That understanding may not sit well or sell well, but it is a fact that will severely challenge our faith as fathers. The Father said it would be so.

FAILING FOR FEAR

Jesus minced no words. He was preparing spiritual sons, His disciples, for His departure, committed to leave a legacy that would last. And so He warned them of that which was to come, whether good or bad, whether uplifting or challenging, whether godly or ungodly. These men with whom He had invested

Himself (like our children) had to be forewarned so that they might be forearmed.

Jesus, sharing the Father's heart just before His crucifixion and resurrection, warned of famines, pestilences, geological upheaval and geopolitical strife that would come, yet He declared these were only "the beginning of sorrows" (Matt. 24:8). The Son of the Father was particularly concerned about the massive deception that would sweep the earth, especially among those who otherwise professed His name, "And because iniquity shall abound, the love of many shall wax cold" (Matt. 24:2). These sober warnings should grip the hearts of fathers today. Any lesser reaction is to hide one's head in the proverbial sand.

Reality is, indeed, coming home to roost for any dad whose heart is truly turned toward the Father and walking as the Son. We are living in those times so graphically described by our Lord. And just how serious are these times, both for us fathers and for those who would follow in our footsteps? Please hear the words of admonition from the Father's heart as declared by His only begotten Son.

And there shall be signs in the sun, and in the moon, and the stars; and upon the earth distress of nations, with perplexity; the sea and the waves roaring;

Men's hearts failing them for fear, and for looking after those things which are coming upon the earth. (Luke 21:25–26)

WHEN CHILDREN FEAR

If the hearts of macho men are "failing them for fear" because of what they see, feel, and hear, how should we fathers expect our young who trust us to respond? This is not hypothetical. To fail to embrace the gravamen of this issue is totally hypocritical. It is nothing short of *playing pretend* with those who have rightfully placed their trust in us as surrogates of the Father.

So . . . as real men . . . as genuine, trustworthy fathers, what should we do? How should we respond amid the unpleasant realities that are now plaguing and will increasingly plague our planet? And what will enable us to come to grips in our own minds and hearts with the truth of increasing trials and tribulations spoken of by prophets, apostles, and the Father through the mouth of Jesus? Such considerations are neither trivial nor to be trifled with but rather to be seriously grafted into our thoughts so as to take hold of our hearts and our practices in our homes.

When children fear, it can have a profound effect upon their faith in the Father and upon their trust in their own fathers.

When children fear, it can have a profound effect upon their faith in the Father and upon their trust in their own fathers. As trials and tribulations increase, trust must rise commensurately or faith will collapse. When true faith collapses, our sons and daughters, whom we deem dear, will be increasingly opened to destiny-changing deceptions that promise to temporarily allay fears and provide false hope. We fathers hold the promise of genuine hope that breeds Christlike courage for such challenging times.

A necessary rhetorical question should even now be arcing in our minds. How am I doing as a father standing in for the Father, in discipling my kids to stand firm in faith in exceedingly troubled times? Or are we, as a family, just continuing in a somewhat passive faith, with little consideration or preparation for the rising tumult throughout our culture and the world? Are we resting our children's future faith on a *PollyAnna* view of life, leaving legacy to just take care of itself, just cavalierly embracing a "Whatever" mind-set? Or, have we wrapped the future of those dear children in a fatalistic blanket expressed so well by the lyrics "Que será, será / whatever will be will be / the future's not mine to see / que será será"?

WHAT SHOULD GODLY FATHERS DO IN FEARFUL TIMES?
BUILD AN ARK OF FAITH

Jesus made clear that as it was in the days of Noah, so shall it be also in the days of the Son of man," or, the days before Christ's return (Luke 17:26). What, then, *was* it like in the days of Noah? It was business as usual, with a terrifying twist. Wickedness was great! Man's thoughts were evil continually. Corruption and violence were rampant (Gen. 6:5, 11–12). Does this not sound suspiciously familiar? Are these not the times in which we are fathering?

Yet, amid the tribulation of the times, the Father found Noah as a faithful and trustworthy father, one who truly "walked with God," was a "just man" and who was "perfect in his generations" (Gen. 6:9). And so Noah "found grace in the eyes of the LORD" to save mankind, his own family, from judgment (Gen. 6:8). The Father then gave Noah, His earthly father surrogate, a faith-filled challenge and calling for troubled times . . . "Build an ark" (Gen. 6:14). And Noah, over the next century, did exactly that, with courage and faith-filled conviction. "Thus did Noah according to all that God commanded him" (Gen. 6:22).

Question: Are you willing to "build an ark" to save your sons and daughters . . . your grandchildren . . . those who trust you as a spiritual "father" in your generation? This may well be the last generation given the opportunity to *build an ark*. What, then, are the building materials for an *ark of faith*?

1. CHRISTLIKE TRUST. In Noah's day, the Messiah had not been revealed, so the Father spoke directly to Noah. In response, Noah did exactly what the word of the Father had instructed . . . he built an ark. Similarly, Jesus, in His day, did the same. He built an ark, not of wood but of faith revealed in obedience. He did only what the Father instructed, because he trusted the Father implicitly. For this reason, Jesus Christ became the sole foundation of our faith, exemplified in loving obedience to the Father's word and will.

Absolute trust revealed in obedience was the hallmark of Christ's life as the Son. His life, death, and resurrection then became the living *ark* of safety for eternal salvation for us and for our sons and daughters.

We, as the Noahs of our day, are to build an ark of faith-filled trust.

We, as the *Noahs* of our day, are to build an ark of faith-filled trust in Christ as the only truly obedient Son, and similarly take the Father's Word as absolute truth upon which we can raise our children in the same unshakable foundation of trust and obedience. Our children are not likely to *enter the ark* with confidence unless they perceive we have done so with absolute confidence.

2. CHRISTLIKE CHARACTER. It is one thing to claim to have built an ark, yet it is quite another to live a life worthy of entering. Undoubtedly many a man worked with Noah and his sons to build the ark, a massive project, but none of them entered the ark. Neither their minds nor their hearts were united with Noah's as to the character of their lives that demanded that the ark be built.

Character counts. The word *character* is one way of expressing the clear connection between what we say we believe and how we live. We refer to a man whose professed belief is not reflected accurately or consistently in his life ways as a *hypocrite*. We say that he lacks *integrity*. The question then haunts our homes . . . what do my children or grandchildren say or think? Is my home truly a safe haven where Christlike character guides and protects purported faith and trust? Our legacy may lie in the balance?

3. CHRISTLIKE COURAGE. Courage is the backbone of moral character. When courage weakens, the spiritual back slumps. One can barely fathom fatherly leadership without courage. Courage links all of moral character and genuine faith into a single operative body that enables a man to "take a stand."

The famous sage Goethe gave us the following words, which should grip our hearts as fathers:

Wealth lost, something lost;

Honor lost, much lost;

Courage lost, all lost.

Are you willing to take a stand? In this evil day, are you doing all to stand, having your loins girt about with truth that does not sway with the tides of cultural feelings or is not enveloped by the tsunamis of godless teachings, even in the name of science, that erode the very foundations of our faith and that of our children? Or will the winds of social pressure, employment compromise, relational infidelity, selfish ambition . . . or fear of loss of ministry funding or constituent support topple your moral frame, allowing onlooking children to see their father falter and fall under such minor trials and tribulation?

William Bentley Ball, a constitutional attorney of renown, prefacing *In Search of a National Morality*, wrote, "Moral courage is that most unfashionable virtue."[1] Indeed it is! On many of the issues that men and fathers face, we lack wisdom because we lack courage.

"A decline in courage may be the most striking feature . . . in our days," observed Aleksandr Solzhenitsyn. "From ancient times decline in courage has been considered the beginning of the end."[2] But we no longer, as fathers, need wander in trepidation and fear. We must take courage.

"From ancient times decline in courage has been considered the beginning of the end." —Aleksandr Solzhenitsyn

---

The Father, in passing the baton of leadership from Moses to Joshua in terrifying times just as the *children* of Israel were to enter the promised land, filled with wicked and fierce warriors, gave these words of exhortation that each of us should closely embrace for our times.

> Be strong and of good courage; be not afraid, neither be thou dismayed: for the LORD thy God is with thee whithersoever thou goest. (Josh. 1:9)

BE BRAVE WITHOUT BRAVADO

The Father is looking to and fro throughout the earth for a few faithful fathers who can and will stand in fearful times. But how do we maintain the courage necessary to brave the tumultuous waves that will increasingly sweep across the hulls of our homes . . . the ark we are building?

Here are seven serious and sobering admonitions that will help us stand bravely, yet without prideful bravado, as we see "the great and terrible day of the LORD" approaching (Joel 2:31).

1. FEAR NOT

The Father repeatedly exhorted His son Israel and all of his children to "fear not." We are told that "God hath not given us the spirit of fear; but of power, and of love, and of a sound mind (2 Tim. 1:7). Fear not man. Neither fear rejection by an increasingly godless culture. As it is written, "The fear of man bringeth a snare, but whoso putteth his trust in the LORD shall be safe" (Prov. 29:25).

"Perfect love casteth our fear." The man who yields to fleshly fear will be tormented. But "there is no fear in love . . . He that feareth is not made perfect in love" (1 John 4:18). The greater our genuine love for the Father, the less our fear of man. The greater our genuine, godly love for our wives and our sons and daughters, the less our fear of the wicked machinations of man. We are enabled then to be fearless and faithful without falling.

2. FRET NOT

Fretting is faithless. Our propensity in the flesh to fret reveals the weakness in our spirit to trust our Father and to live by faith.

Fretting actually frustrates faith. And a father's fretting in the face of his family is a declaration to both wife and children of the serious weakness of his alleged faith. For this reason, we are exhorted by the psalmist David, "Fret not thyself because of evildoers" (Ps. 37:1).

Our children need to see us victorious in faith.

Our flesh will always demand that we fret. This helps us to understand the nature of spiritual warfare. It is a continual battle, this conflict between the flesh and the spirit. And our children need to see us victorious in faith.

3. FALL NOT

Falling, alone and in an isolated instance, does not define or determine *failing*. But persistent falling reveals a propensity to fail, which seriously impairs hope for a godly, lasting legacy.

As fathers holding the Father's treasure of gospel hope in earthen vessels, we occasionally will stumble and sometimes fall (2 Cor. 3:7). Yet, in our seeming weakness, by the Father's grace (enabling power and favor) we can be restored and made strong. It is always a matter of the heart. And we are called to be overcomers (Rev. 2–3).

The classic film *Chariots of Fire* drives this message home and to the heart for every sincere father. Eric Liddell, the focus of the film, finds himself in a dire circumstance as "Scotland's fastest wing." He is challenged to run a particular race to display his running prowess but is tripped up by an unscrupulous competitor, causing Eric to stumble and fall, seeming to doom him to failure. And the movie captures the moment so that every man viewing must himself enter the mind and heart of this young man as he weighs, in an instant, how to respond. Should he quit . . . or should he rise again to the race set before him?

Empowered and inspired by the Father's favor and amazing grace, Eric rolls on the track with the momentum of the moment, rises, shakes himself, and passionately pursues the race set before him until gloriously he crosses the finish line, having prevailed against all odds, to the glory of God. The gravity of the true account based on the life of a truly God-loving and Father-fearing young man should grip the heart of every father and compel him to finish well. Watch it again . . . and again . . . yes, with your children at your side. It is pure, and it is passionate!

Regretfully, there is a falling unto final failure and eternal loss. It involves a persistent "falling away" (2 Thess. 2:3; Heb. 6:6). Such *falling away* leads not only to personal perdition but to destruction of paternal legacy. For this reason we are given dire warning.

Falling away leads not only to personal perdition but to destruction of paternal legacy.

Fortunately, the Father is able to "keep us from falling" if we truly and sincerely follow His Word, Will and Ways (Jude 24). When we "fall into temptation," we are to "count it all joy" because our faith is being tested so that we might be perfected (James 1:2–4). We are to "submit to God" . . . and only then "resist the devil," who will "flee from you" (4:7). We are to "draw nigh to God [the Father]" and then "He will draw nigh to you" (4:8).

Grace is not a prescription to sin promiscuously but rather a provision to keep us from falling. We are warned to flee temptation, especially sexual sin (1 Cor. 6:18) and the "love of money" (1 Tim. 6:9–11). Can I, as a husband and father, claim with a straight face that I am submitted to the Father when I am perpetually seduced by porn or by greed? "Let him that thinketh he standeth take heed lest he fall" (1 Cor. 10:12).

Remember! "There hath no temptation taken you but such as is common to man: but God is faithful . . . [and] will with the temptation also make a way to escape…" " Now all these things . . . are written for our admonition, upon whom the ends of the world are come" so, take heed lest you fall (1 Cor. 10:13, 11–12).

The apostle Peter gave us a detailed prescription as to how we might prevail in these progressively evil times. We have devoted the entire chapter 15 to applying his prescription based upon the promises of the Father. Let us remind ourselves of his final admonition:

Wherefore the rather brethren, give diligence to make your calling and election sure: for if ye do these things, ye shall never fall. (2 Peter 1:10)

Remember this! "A just man falleth seven times, and riseth up again, but the wicked shall fall into mischief" (Prov. 24:16).

4. FORGET NOT

How easy it is for us as men to forget. Over and over the Father, through His Word, admonishes us not to forget but to remember. And if there was ever a time that we desperately need to embrace this warning and encouragement, it is today.

Here is a sampling of that which our Father would have us not forget.

> Take heed . . . lest ye forget the covenant of the LORD your God. (Deut. 4:23)

> Beware that thou forget not the LORD thy God, in not keeping his commandments. (Deut. 8:11)

> If thou do at all forget the LORD your God . . . I testify . . . that ye shall surely perish. (Deut. 8:19–20)

The flip side of the Father's warning to "forget not" is His exhortation to "Remember." In order to forget not, we fathers must purpose to *remember* and practice *remembering*, both for ourselves and for our families.

We fathers must purpose to remember and practice remembering.

> Remember now thy Creator, in the days of thy [relative] youth. (Eccl. 12:1). This may be one of your children's deepest defenses against the godless evolutionary doctrines.

> Remember all the commandments of the LORD. (Num. 15:39)

Remember the Sabbath day, to keep it holy. (Ex. 20:8)

Remember . . . from whence thou art fallen. (Rev. 2:5)

Stir up your . . . minds by way of remembrance. (2 Peter 3:1)

Remember Lot's wife. (Luke 17:32)

Frivolously spent time and addictive technology are thieves we grant entrance into our homes to steal our family focus, disrupt our family faith and destroy our family joy and protection by cauterizing our memories, rendering them insensitive both to the Word of the Lord and to remembrance of His mighty acts.

Remembering is the Father's affirmative action program for all fathers. It is the only antidote to the deadly poison of forgetting in an increasingly faithless world. And we must remember out loud to our sons and daughters.

5. FEAR THE LORD

We have already discussed this in depth, but "by way of remembrance," perhaps we should be reminded that the fear of the Lord is foundational to fathering if we are to have hope of a godly legacy that will last. This is especially true in fearful times.

"In the fear of the LORD is strong confidence . . . [providing] a place of refuge" (Prov. 14:26). "The fear of the LORD is a fountain of life," enabling us and our families "to depart from the snares of death" (Prov. 14:27). The Father will teach the fathers who truly *fear the Lord* (Ps. 25:12).

"In the fear of the Lord is strong confidence . . . [providing] a place of refuge." —Prov. 14:26

There is great security and peace for fathers who truly *fear the Lord*. In fact, "The secret of the LORD is with them that fear him; and he will shew them his covenant" (Ps. 25:14). The *fear of the Lord* protects us and our families from "the fear of man" (Heb. 13:6; Ps. 56:11), because the "fear of man" is a snare . . . a trap . . . for our children (Prov. 29:25). And the *fear of the Lord* enables us to both identify and hate evil (Prov. 8:13).

Amid fearful times, the man who truly fears the Lord "shall not be afraid of evil tidings: his heart is fixed, trusting in the LORD. His heart is established, he shall not be afraid" (Ps. 112:7–8). Men must seriously reconsider the Father's covenant with those who both love and fear Him.

> Blessed is the man that *feareth the LORD*, that delighteth greatly in his commandments. His seed shall be mighty upon the earth: the generation of the upright shall be blessed. (Ps. 112:1–2)

Wisdom begins with the *fear of the Lord*, enabling us as men and fathers to have greater understanding as we follow Father's commandments (Ps. 111:10). Do we not need exceptional wisdom and understanding in which our sons and daughters can find hope and confidence in these troubled times?

(Note: A more complete understanding of the

all-encompassing role of the fear of the Lord in your life, can be found in my book *The Secret of the Lord*, Elijah Books, 2011.)

6. FOLLOW FAITHFULLY

If we, as fathers, are not able to faithfully follow the Father, who changes not, how can we expect our children to follow us in security and confidence? To be a father who leads to a promised legacy, I must first be a follower of the Father who made the promise. But what does it mean to be a follower? Is it cognitive assent to religious facts, or is it rather a way of life that conforms to the ways of the Father's household . . . as the Father alone defines those ways?

How closely do I follow the one I claim to be my Father? In Christ's most troubled and trying hour, all of his professed disciples either fled or followed "afar off" (Matt. 26:56, 58). Following demands extreme faith in fearful times. How, then, should we understand what it means to *follow* in fearful times? Here is just a brief glimpse as to the implications of the gospel for fathers who would have godly followers.

Following demands extreme faith in fearful times.

FOLLOW RIGHTEOUSNESS. "But thou, O man of God, flee these things [that cause to err from faith [listed in I Tim. 6:3–10]; and *follow after righteousness*, godliness, faith, love, patience, meekness (1 Tim. 6:11; see also 2 Tim. 2:22).

FOLLOW HOLINESS, "without which no man shall see the Lord. . . . Lift up your hands which hand down, and the feeble knees; And make straight paths for your feet" (Heb. 12:14, 12–13, see also 1 Peter 1:13–16).

FOLLOW CHRIST'S SUFFERING. "For even hereunto were ye called: because Christ also suffered for us, leaving us an example, that ye should *follow in his steps*" (1 Peter 2:21).

> "Forasmuch then as Christ hath suffered for us in the flesh, arm yourselves likewise with the same mind: for he that hath suffered in the flesh hath ceased from sin; That he no longer should live the rest of his time in the flesh to the lust of men, but to the will of God" (1 Peter 4:1–2).

> "Beloved [fathers], think it not strange concerning the fiery trial which is to try you, as though some strange thing happened unto you: But rejoice, inasmuch as you are partakers of Christ's sufferings" (1 Peter 4:12–13).

FOLLOW STEWARDSHIP. "It is required in stewards, that a man be found faithful" (1 Cor. 4:2). As fathers, we are appointed stewards of our children by the Father. We are the Father's surrogates—His hand extended—to raise, nurture, and guide our young on behalf of the Father, both in Spirit and in truth.

All of the assets and income within our domain belong to the Father. We are trustees, delegated by the Father to use these for His glory and for the advancement of His kingdom, beginning with our families. Our talents and gifts are held by us in trust to do the Father's will. But do our children and grandchildren believe that? Do they see it borne out in our lives? It is difficult to remember in a world dedicated to SELF that our very lives are an investment by the Father in the future kingdom of His Son.

FOLLOW WITHOUT FAIL. "Be thou *faithful unto death*, and I will give thee a crown of life" (Rev. 2:10).

Faithfulness in following is tested in the crucible of fearful times. Our children need to learn such faithfulness both by fatherly precept and fatherly example.

Faithfulness in following is tested in the crucible of fearful times.

Growing up as a young boy, I was taught a simple yet profound truth through the life of the prophet Daniel. Daniel, together with his three Hebrew friends, were taken captive as young men, probably in their teens. In Babylon, they were surrounded by a godless and idolatrous culture that threatened to press them into its mold. That pressure ultimately threatened each of them with their very lives. Would they be faithful . . . or not?

Out of this fearful environment of consummate testing came the simple lyrics of a little song . . .

DARE to be a Daniel,

DARE to stand alone,

DARE to have a purpose firm, and

DARE to make it known.

My young life was deeply impressed by these words that have strengthened me throughout my life in difficult times. I taught them to my daughters, and they were similarly gripped, so that when my firstborn grandson was born, he was named Daniel. I designed and presented to Daniel a special calligraphed plaque, and the beautifully presented lyrics of that song have become a lasting legacy.

Several years ago I had the privilege of speaking at a celebratory event for the largest Christian school in Ghana, Africa. Five hundred or so students ages five to nineteen were gathered, and I exhorted each of them to "dare to be a Daniel" with those simple lyrics made memorable by the melody. Over and over throughout the assembly, they repeated and sang those faith-building words that united the hearts of all ages into a ringing chorus of conviction. I was told years later that many were still singing and molded toward faithfulness by that chorus.

The accuser of our children is alive and well. The deceiver seeks to destroy them daily. And we must teach them to be overcomers—even if threatened with death, as Daniel was—by our faithful example. As it is written . . .

> And they overcame him by the blood of the Lamb, and by the word of their testimony; *and they loved not their lives unto the death.* (Rev. 12:11–12)

7. FIGHT THE GOOD FIGHT

We are at war, dads! As fathers and grandfathers, we are called by the Father to stand, and having done all to stand, to still stand. We must stand! Our children are trusting us to remain true . . . even unto death. But we can only do that by "put[ting] on the whole armour of God" daily, "that ye may be able to stand against the wiles of the devil" (Eph. 6:10–11). We must be lovers of the Father's truth, girding it about the most vulnerable areas of our lives.

We are at war, dads! Our children are trusting us to remain true . . . even unto death.

This will demand a level of dedication seldom seen in the Western world in our generation. It will require a depth of prayer, watchfulness and perseverance rarely practiced among professing Christian men today (Eph. 6:18). It will demand that, in the force of profound and discouraging adversity, we "cast not away . . . [our] confidence, which hath great recompense of reward For [we] have need of patience, that, after [we] have done the will of God, [we] might receive the promise" (Heb. 10:35–36).

It is time for fathers to get into the battle and "fight the good fight of faith" (1 Tim. 6:12). What will you say when you face the ultimate, existential moment of your life, when you have done all you could do, said all you could say, lived all you could to define the destiny of those who will follow? Consider the convicting words of a former murderer who, in his moment of truth and knocked off his "high horse," radically committed his life to leaving an eternal legacy that lasts to this day. Having changed his name from Saul—the religious murderer—to Paul the apostle, he declared as he faced death for his faith these challenging words for all who would follow.

I have fought a good fight, I have finished my course, I have kept the faith: Henceforth there is laid up for me a crown of righteousness, which the Lord, the righteous judge, shall give me at that day: *and not to me only, but unto all them also that love his appearing.* (2 Tim. 4:7–8)

May all who come behind us find us faithful, like Paul!

PROBING OUR HEARTS

1. Why will men's hearts *fail for fear* in these end times in which we live?

2. Has the significance of these "latter days" gripped your fatherly heart yet? Why . . . or why not?

3. In what ways are you preparing your kids to stand firm in faith as the times become even more troubled?

4. How can you, like Noah, build an *ark of faith* for your family amid a mocking culture? Have you started building yet? What have you done? If you were to be tried . . . or fired as a builder of faith as a father, would an objective employer (God) hire . . . or fire you?

5. Has any warning or wooing exhortation stood out to you, in particular, as you considered these fearful times?

21

THE FATHER'S BLESSING

When a father understands the redemptive power of the blessing, he will take the time to impart blessings to his children on a regular basis.
—BILL LIGON, *IMPARTING THE BLESSING*

A FATHER'S BLESSING is without earthly substitute. A child not blessed by the father is a child in quiet, yet painful bereavement. For absence of the father's blessing betrays one of a father's greatest duties and abandons a child to bemoan for a lifetime the emptiness of soul arising from lack of the father's affirmation.

SEEKING A BLESSING

Every child yearns to be blessed by a loving father. Adult *children*, regardless of age or status, secretly seek for the open and spoken affirmation that should proceed periodically from the lips of every loving father. When, over time, the inward yearning and expectation is not fulfilled, a vacuum is created in the spirit that is often filled by other destiny-determining influences that either divert or destroy any desired legacy.

Every child yearns to be blessed by a loving father.

Unwelcome and ungodly suitors invade a daughter's life, filling the vacancy left by absence of either the father's presence or blessing. Statistics make clear the profound interconnection between unwed pregnancy and the void left in a daughter's soul through fatherly disconnect. Young men also pursue substitutes for a dad's presence or promise, often drugs or gangs, or even homosexuality.

Seekers will find something to satisfy the deep, inner cry of the soul. They will find it either with dad or with destructive influences and behaviors, which some refer to as *acting out*. When a father either fails or selfishly refuses to provide both a secure presence and a sense of blessing, over time, the child is prone to wander and even outright reject the Father, leaving an eternal void readily filled by the deceiver. Legacy languishes for lack of a father's active and pro-active love.

BLESSING IS NOT BANAL

True blessing is borne of the Father by His Spirit. It is not banal, boring, repetitive, mindless, and ultimately meaningless. Blessing is not the issuance of meaningless or manipulative words. Rather, blessing is a profound articulation of the deepest recesses of a father's heart toward his sons and daughters. Grandfathers, likewise, are called to both be a blessing and to proclaim blessing.

Grandfathers are called to both be a blessing and to proclaim blessing.

Blessing is a great privilege bestowed by the Father to us. It may well be our ultimate calling. By blessing our progeny, we actually bless the Lord, who entrusted them to us that we might care for them on His behalf.

BLESSED TO BE A BLESSING

Consider the "father of the faith." His name was Abraham. Because of his great faith, trusting the Father, the Father returned the blessing, declaring:

> And I will make of thee a great nation; and *I will bless thee*, and make thy name great; and *thou shalt be a blessing*. (Gen. 12:2)

Notice the temporal and eternal pattern . . . blessed to be a blessing. The foundation of a father's blessing is the manner in which he trains his children. Listen carefully and ponder the Father's further blessing of Abraham . . . a promise to serve the Father's intentions to his son of faith.

> All the nations of the earth shall be blessed in him . . . For I know him, that he shall command his children and his household after him, and they shall keep the way of the

LORD, to do justice and judgment; that the LORD may bring upon Abraham [bless him with] that which he hath spoken. (Gen. 18:17–19)

Be encouraged! Abraham was not a perfect father, yet he set his heart to both obey and fear the Lord (Gen. 22:12). His very life blessed his children, grandchildren, great-grandchildren, and through them, even the nations. And so the Father repeated His blessing to his faithful son . . .

And in thy seed shall all the nations be blessed; because thou hast obeyed my voice. (Gen. 22:18)

Words are cheap. Yet with our Father, words have great power, even the power to determine destiny and define legacy. A life of obedience sets the stage for the Father's blessing in our fatherly lives. It is the greatest of all blessings we can bestow upon our descendants, but it must also be communicated with heartfelt words.

Words have great power, even the power to determine destiny and define legacy.

A pastor once said, "Faith is a long obedience in the same direction." Indeed it is! As it is written:

And Abraham was old, and well stricken in age: and the LORD [Father] had *blessed Abraham in all things* (Gen. 24:1).

Abraham's blessing, both in prophetic words and follow-up-actions by the Father, echoes into the next two generations.

And it came to pass after the death of Abraham, that God [the Father] *blessed his son Isaac* (Gen. 25:11).

And the LORD appeared unto him . . . and said, I am the God of Abraham thy father: fear not, for I am with thee, and *will bless thee*, and multiply thy seed *for my servant Abraham's sake* (Gen. 26:24).

Notice! The son's blessing was the legacy of his father's long obedience in the same direction—his faith.

Then appears Jacob, Abraham's second-born grandson. The firstborn grandson was Esau, who did not value the eternal firstborn legacy of either his father or grandfather, but was willing to barter it away to his brother for "a mess of pottage" to satisfy his temporary hunger. Only when, at the end of his father Isaac's life, he realized the consequence of having bartered away his blessing, did Esau experience weeping remorse and a sense of unmeasurable loss. And so he cried out pitifully to his father, "Hast thou not reserved a blessing for me?" (Gen. 27:36).

How many men, sons of their fathers, have cried deeply with tears of the soul, "Have you not reserved a blessing for me?" Or, perhaps more poignantly and pertinently, "Why have you never spoken or secured in your heart a place of blessing for me?" Such anguish of soul of many sons and daughters is palpable. And lamentably, many a father will pay the eternal price.

The blessing of the fathers endures to the third and fourth generation—and even beyond. And so Jacob, Abraham's grandson, received the echoing blessing of his grandfather, fulfilling in three generations the Father's promised blessing that would continue echoing on through time until the Second Coming of the Father's "only begotten Son." And the Father said to Jacob:

Thy name shall be called no more Jacob, but Israel: for a prince hast thou power with God and with men, and hast prevailed. (Gen. 32:28)

What will enable our sons, daughters and grandchildren to *prevail* in this wicked and perverse generation in which a genuine legacy of faith is rejected in favor of the love of a fleeting temporal legacy? The answer may well lie in the hearts and blessing of the fathers.

THE POWER OF WORDS

Words count! A father's words can produce faith or folly. A father's words can breed hope or horror and can provide direction or lead to destruction.

Words are seeds. They eventually produce after their kind. Over time, a child's life is largely directed and defined by the seeds of the father's mouth. Those seeds germinate in seeming darkness, yet when they begin to emerge, they mature into a blessing or a curse. And, largely unbeknownst to us, they reseed themselves, multiplying blessing or cursing in our homes and families.

With words our Father, through His Son, spoke the worlds into existence (Heb. 11:3). He upholds all things through "the word of his power" (Heb. 1:1–3). And in a much more limited sense, the Father has bestowed upon us as men, created in His image, the creative or destructive power of words.

The Father's concern related to the words of our mouth are woven throughout both Old and New Testaments. Words of distrust, murmuring and unbelief kept all but two of the six hundred thousand adult males the Father had delivered from the bondage of Egypt from entering the promised land (Num. 14:26–38). Their children, lamentably, bore much of the brunt of their father's faithless words, causing them to wander in life's wilderness for forty years (Num. 14:33).

How many of our children and grandchildren have wandered aimlessly . . . and even destructively . . . for want of a faithful father's words? America is now ravaged by an entire generation of wandering and faithless sons and daughters whose parents, while going to church, never seemed to grasp the significance of selfish lives and self-blessing words, launching the "ME, ME, ME" generation. Indeed, the words we speak, or don't speak, have immense power to produce after their kind; for better or for ill.

Words weigh heavily and reflect our hearts. As Jesus declared, "Out of the abundance of the heart the mouth speaketh" (Matt. 12:34). For this reason we are warned that "every idle word that men shall speak, they shall give account thereof in the day of judgment. For by thy words thou shalt be justified, and by thy words thou shalt be condemned" (Matt. 12:36–37).

The apostle James gave powerful focus to both the blessing and cursing consequences of our tongues (James 3). "Out of the same mouth proceedeth blessing and cursing. My brethren, these things ought not so to be" (v. 10). On the contrary, the book of Proverbs tells us that "a word fitly spoken is like apples of gold in pictures of silver" (25:11), but "a fool's mouth is his destruction, and his lips are the snare of his soul" (18:7). "Death and life are in the power of the tongue: and they that love it shall eat the fruit thereof" (18:21).

What fruit are we feeding our sons and daughters through the words of our mouth? Their perception is their reality. Are we sowing words of faith or of frustration? Do our words build, or destroy? Will the seedlings of our sayings produce confidence or perpetual condemnation? Do we flatter, or do we instill realistic hope and life-sustaining faith?

A FAMILY BLESSING

A truly blessed family is a family blessed by the father. A father's lasting blessing is born out of a life lived in consistent harmony with the ways of the Father, coupled with honest, godly and vision-casting words as if issuing straight from the Father's own mouth.

Every family needs, even craves, the father's blessing as if spoken through the Father himself. Our children and our wives live in a parched and thirsty land without the persistent and passionate blessing of dad and husband. Many a legacy languishes for lack of the father's blessing.

> A truly blessed family is a family blessed by the father.

Congregations, as large and extended families of faith, likewise crave a consistent blessing, even amid times of needed correction. The Father well knew this and commanded Moses that Aaron and his sons (as priests, pastors, spiritual fathers) bless the children of Israel. I well remember the timeless blessing pronounced by my own father, as pastor, over his longing congregation, thus perpetuating in time the Aaronic Benediction.

The LORD bless thee, and keep thee:

The LORD make his face shine upon thee, and be gracious unto thee:

The LORD lift up his countenance upon thee, and give thee peace. (Num. 6:24–26)

The purpose of the blessing was that the priests or pastors "put my name upon the children of Israel; and I will bless them" (Num. 6:27).

BLESSED—AND A BLESSING

A true blessing is both creative and carries profound conviction: From the Father's blessing of Abraham, the *father of our faith* to the blessing of Jesus, son of Abraham by faith and Son of the Father, a blessing was ordained that those who are so blessed should *be a blessing*. It is such a blessing out of which legacy is formed and brings forth a life-giving future.

This matter of the father's blessing now becomes intensely personal, for a father's blessing is not only for families, congregations, and even nations, but more importantly for individuals. It is in the personal and individual blessing that legacy is intensified and given explicit expression. It is for this reason that the more prominent blessings bestowed by fathers throughout Scripture are seen as prophetic in nature. They define the course of destiny.

Rhetorical questions are thus thrust deeply into our fatherly minds and hearts. Am I a blessing to my wife and family? What do they think? What does the Father think? How are the words of my mouth working? What is the fruit? Do I have such a father's heart as gleaned from my own deep, communicating relationship with the Father that I can see His hand upon my sons and daughters . . . grandchildren . . . and specifically bless them accordingly, without flattery?

A HOPE AND A FUTURE

A father's legacy languishes for lack of blessing from his father. Similarly, our children's future is often stagnated by absence of specific blessing from dad.

God the Father well understood this unique and necessary power of specific blessing. He demonstrated it in serious simplicity in the deputizing of His only begotten Son. The power of that blessing has brought hope and salvation to the world—an unending eternally enduring legacy.

A father's legacy languishes for lack of blessing from his father.

As to Israel, the Father's adopted son, even after serious fatherly correction, the eternal Father made clear His ultimate, overarching blessing, which even we, as Gentiles, joyfully embrace.

> For I know the thoughts that I think toward you, saith the LORD, thoughts of peace and not of evil, to give you an expected end [a hope and a future]." (Jer. 29:11)

THE FATHER'S TIMELY BLESSING

Timing is everything! And to discern the appropriate time for the father's blessings may serve either to appoint . . . or disappoint . . . desired legacy.

Consider the life of the Son of God. At His baptism, the Father, through the agency of His Spirit, placed the divine imprimatur upon His Son, declaring:

Thou art my beloved Son; in thee I am well pleased. (Luke 3:22)

That blessing and fatherly affirmation was not bestowed upon the Father's Son until age thirty (Luke 3:23). The timing was crucial and the consequences eternal. Imagine the loss to hope and history had those simple, yet simply profound words not been spoken. Yet lamentably, even Christian fathers today have seemingly no clue as to the echoing consequences of their failure to genuinely bless their sons and daughters.

Interestingly, the Father's blessing of His Son was not complete at Jesus' baptism. The greater blessing remained yet to be spoken, confirming for all time the delegated authority of the Father to His Son. That further blessing remained for the propitious moment described as the *transfiguration* (Luke 9:28–35).

Jesus' most loyal and faithful followers—Peter, James and John—were with Him on a mountain to pray. Suddenly, Jesus was transfigured by the Father in a glistening glory joined by Moses and Elijah, the greatest prophets in Israel's history. And then came the Father's voice out of the glory, aloud saying . . .

"This is my beloved Son: hear him." (Luke 9:35)

Few fathers bless their sons and daughters, calling them *blessed*. Fewer still declare of their children entrusted to them by the Father that they are well pleasing in their father's sight. But precious few indeed even hear the father's passing of the baton of the father's authoritative blessing declaring, "Hear ye him."

It is precisely this final mantle of holy mission and historical purpose that eludes our sons and daughters, leaving them to languish in unmeasurable, and often unwitting, emptiness while seeking in frustration to follow the Father's leading without the express affirmative blessing of their own fathers.

HERITAGE ALONE IS NOT ENOUGH

Consider the enormity of the Father's words in openly affirming His Son. Why were words necessary? After all, did Jesus not recognize His Sonship? Had it not become known to Him, from the miraculous story of His birth to the age of accountability, from bar mitzvah to becoming a grown man, that He was of divine pedigree? Did he not develop an unusual relationship with the Father even as the Son trod planet Earth for thirty years? Why, then, were words of specific blessing needed?

Regardless of pedigree or heritage, a father's pointed blessing is essential to propel, with power, a son or daughter into life's greater calling and purpose. It is by such words that the Spirit of the Father is invested by a father into his children, merging heritage and hope for a future of holy passion and purpose. For lack of such blessing, despite a seeming *godly* heritage, many a child has wandered aimlessly for a lifetime, often taking the path of the prodigal. Many a pastor's child can relate to such a fractured legacy.

A father's pointed blessing is essential to propel, with power, a son or daughter into life's greater calling and purpose.

Heritage alone is not enough to establish or pass on a father's blessing! Allow a window to be opened into my own life. Truly, as the firstborn son of a father who pastored for more than fifty years, such a blessing would seem to be a natural outcome of relationship. Consider also that grandfathers on both mother's and father's sides were also pastors. Such would seem to define a legacy pregnant with holy purpose. But that is only one side of the coin of legacy. Fulfilled legacy cries for the father's blessing.

Painful awareness of this profound need for a father's blessing leapt into our family's life one Father's Day. My parents came to our home for a warm family experience to honor my father. After dinner, we all gathered in the family room to share memories. As we went around the room, each of us was to share some insight or blessing about his or her father. My father was at the end of the circle. And when it became his turn, there was a very lengthy, uncomfortable, and pregnant silence: He could draw nothing from the well of his soul or memory. At long last, grasping for something to say of a truth, he lamentably uttered, "He was steadfast." Steadfastness is commendable—even necessary—but it is no substitute for personal blessing that engenders the deepest of gratitude. My father had pastored for decades with a gaping, unfilled hole in his heart for lack of his father's blessing.

Despite a pastoral heritage, I must confess no awareness that any of my aunts or uncles, all sons and daughters of pastors, ever were the beneficiaries of their father's blessing. Apparently, such blessing was merely presumed, yet never performed, whether for sons or daughters. A pity!

My pastoral parents always were convinced their eldest son would likewise be a pastor or otherwise dedicated to a customary "full-time Christian ministry." After nine years of public school teaching, twenty years of law practice while teaching principles of the Kingdom as a businessman and lawyer, and two political campaigns for the California legislature, the Lord spoke to my heart at forty-eight years of age that I was to leave the practice of law at the height of my career, leave thirty years of business, political and ministry investment, sell all, and remove from California to the birthplace of America on the shores of the James River, where the cross of the covenant was first planted in 1607. The Father had spoken shockingly and deeply that "you have been pleading the cause of men long enough; I want you now to plead My cause in the land as a Voice to the Church, declaring Vision to the Nation." My simple answer was "Yes, Sir!"

In 1992 we formed Save America Ministries as "A Voice to the Church, declaring Vision to the Nation" for the express purpose of "Rebuilding the Foundations of Faith and Freedom." But something was missing. I became painfully aware that I had never received my father's blessing or even open affirmation. I felt paralyzed to proceed. And it was increasingly painful. What to do? Somehow I needed to reach my father's heart, but how? Need a son beg for a blessing?

> Somehow, I needed to reach my father's heart, but how? Need a son beg for a blessing?

An idea struck. I would invite my pastor-dedicated father to share a couple of short weekend forays. And so we got together at two of California's renowned vacation spots, one at Lake Arrowhead in the mountains and one at Palm Springs. During these short father-son encounters, I attempted to seek out my father's heart as to what my wife and I were now doing in America's greatest crisis hour. I longed desperately to hear his deeply embracing words of affirmation, yet his lips seemed sealed. The void in my spirit seemed to widen as a great chasm yearning to be filled.

It was in Palm Springs that we again created the time to connect. It seemed this would be the last opportunity. Yet again, no response. What is it that ties a man's tongue that he cannot . . . or will not . . . embrace and affirm his son—especially when that son is openly fulfilling the parents' professed hope and dream?

No hint would suffice. And so, with deep masculine emotion, restrained but obvious, I blurted out, "Dad, I have become deeply aware of a great void in my life. I have embarked on a tremendous faith journey at the command of the Father, but I have never received my own father's blessing. Never, Dad. Never!"

He was painfully dumbfounded, presuming apparently that whatever favorable thoughts he may have entertained in his own mind would somehow telepathically communicate to mine. It was hard to fault him because he had never received or known of such a blessing from his own father. And then, in few and somewhat faltering words, yet with strength of a man of deep conviction, the long-sought blessing poured forth, and I became a true man—free in a new and powerful way—to do the Father's will.

The release and joy to this day are nearly inexpressible. My father's heart was truly turned toward mine. Now mine could be even more deeply turned toward him and return to the Father's heart with an even greater and more seemingly secure full force of faith. And that is now a lasting legacy transmitted to many that the hearts of millions of fathers may be turned toward their children and the hearts of the children turned toward their fathers.

PROBING OUR HEARTS

1. What is a blessing? To what extent and why do you think that a father's blessing is important?

2. In what ways can a father's words produce either faith or folly . . . with hope or even horror?

3. Why is it that so many young people seem to wander aimlessly? Do you think that lack of a father's faithful words might often be at the root of a child's sense of lostness and lack of direction?

4. Have you ever intentionally, from your heart, blessed your children or your family?

5. What was your reaction to the author's personal story?

22

DESTINY BEGINS TODAY

Generally, godly children come from godly homes where godly fathers live godly lives.

—STEVEN LAWSON, *THE LEGACY*

DELAY IS NOT AN OPTION for a dad determined to leave a lasting legacy. Every successful father well knows that tomorrows are largely defined by what happens today.

THE POWER OF PROCRASTINATION

We are all prone to procrastination—don't do today what you can put off until tomorrow. Yet procrastination, as a persistent habit of mind and heart, of will and emotions, is powerful and pernicious. It is deadly if one is concerned about the destiny of our children.

Procrastination for a father is a prescription for failure. For such a father, the future never seems to seriously connect to today or this week. The future is always elusive. Dismissed from mind and heart is the looming reality that the future will one day, perhaps soon, become the present—a present defined by a promiscuous or persistent procrastination.

This power of procrastination can be readily seen and even measured in many *secular* areas of our lives, whether in delay in savings or investment, failure to timely pay bills, deferred maintenance of our houses, or even in deferred care for our spouses. But in no area of our lives is procrastination deadlier or of greater lasting effect than in our *spiritual* lives and in the godly training and touching of our children and grandchildren. Since it is well said that *God has no grandchildren*, today defines destiny for this generation—your generation and mine.

Since God has no grandchildren, today defines destiny for this generation.

THE PROFICIENT PROCRASTINATOR

It is easy for a man to develop a proficiency in procrastination, where it becomes an actual life practice. Such *proficiency* is developed like any other proficiency—choice after choice, use after use, delay after delay, until it has become, as it were, a noxious poison deadening the mental, emotional and spiritual faculties of a father to make decisions that will define tomorrow.

Tomorrow, therefore, is seen to *merely happen*, and we shrug our shoulders as if we had no real participating role in the devastation left in the wake of our indecision. Such thinking has, lamentably, increasingly defined the attitudes and actions of Christian fathers when it comes to consideration of leaving a godly and lasting legacy.

RATIONALIZING THE IRRATIONAL

Have you noticed how easy it is to rationalize or justify whatever it is we want to do . . . or not do . . . at the moment? What is it in our minds and hearts as dads that leads us day after day to make decisions that do not inure to leaving a godly legacy for our kids? Why would we persistently choose work over working with our children? What causes us to turn on the TV continually when our children desperately need dad's presence and attention? Who stands in the way of our leading in daily family meals, without any technological distraction or interference? What prevents us from daily discipleship of our children, including intentional instruction from the Scriptures?

Persistent choices define what we really value.

These choices are all the product of rationalization, aren't they? Painfully, these persistent choices also define what we *really* value. Unfortunately, these collective rationalizations lie at the very heart of deception. And no man is ever deceived against his will. Such self-imposed deceptions are therefore actually defining daily the course of destiny, both for us as fathers and for those who would follow after us.

Destiny Lies Just Ahead

These are ultimate times! We fathers now live in the final, defining moments of history from the Father's viewpoint. And that is why He lovingly, yet with warning, is wooing us to decisively turn our hearts back to Him with diligence so that our children and children's children may follow our lead, anticipating with confidence an everlasting legacy of eternal life.

Delay is not an option! Destiny lies just ahead. And we, as fathers are called to the Kingdom for such a time as this.

Can you hear the Father's pleading voice? Will you heed His call?

Your children await your answer.

PROBING OUR HEARTS

1. Do you tend to be a procrastinator?

2. If God has no grandchildren, what might the implications be for my fatherhood right now?

3. Do you agree that self-imposed deceptions through rationalization are actually defining your children's destiny every day?

4. What kind of rationalizations do you find yourself using to avoid doing the simple things the Father would have you do as a father to leave a spiritual legacy?

5. Can you hear or discern the Father's voice wooing . . . reaching out to you . . . to seriously return unto Him and to turn your heart, as the Father's heart, to your children? Do you think delay is an option?

lingering lines for lasting legacy

"*The heart of a father is the masterpiece of nature.*"

—ABBÉ PRÉVOST

"*Children are gifts. They are not ours for the breaking. They are ours for the making.*"

—DON PEARCE

"*Failure is not final for fathers as long as there is the grace of God [His favor and enabling power].*

—STEVEN LAWSON, *THE LEGACY*

"*Being a great father is like shaving. No matter how good you shaved today, you have to do it again tomorrow.*"

—REED MARKHAM

"*Fathers must stand tall on their knees.*"

—UNKNOWN

"*It's easier to bend a boy than to mend a man.*"

—ANONYMOUS

"*If [fathers] continuously rescue their children, they run the risk of side-lining or benching them from life.*"

—DAN SEABORN, *PARENTING WITH GRACE AND TRUTH*

"A crisis managed well is a blessing in disguise."
—DAN SEABORN, *PARENTING WITH GRACE AND TRUTH*

"A daughter needs a dad to be the standard against which she will judge all men."

—UNKNOWN AUTHOR

"Parenting isn't for cowards."
—DAN SEABORN, *PARENTING WITH GRACE AND TRUTH*

"Don't worry that children never listen to you; worry that they are always watching you."

—ROBERT FULGHUM

"If we're really honest, we make time for what we value."
—MELISSA SPOELSTRA, *TOTAL FAMILY MAKEOVER*

"Only in returning to me and resting in me will you be saved. In quietness and confidence is your strength."

—ISAIAH 30:15 NLT

"The overriding question of biblical prophecy isn't how the world is going to end. Instead, the big question is: How are you going to finish?"
—DAVID SANFORD
(FORWARD OF *SPIRITUAL PREPPER* BY JAKE MCCANDLESS)

"Your children need a godly grandparent—the spiritual legacy you have been passing down to your children."

—JAKE MCCANDLESS

"We will come to our knees, either by choice or by circumstance."
—DOUG STRINGER, *LEADERSHIP AWAKENING*

"At least six other ships warned the Titanic about icebergs in its path. But the captain refused to heed the warnings."
—DOUG STRINGER, *LEADERSHIP AWAKENING*

"The mission field begins in the homes of believing moms and dads."
—JOHN TRENTHAM, TIMOTHY PAUL JONES

"Come out from among them [the world], and be ye separate, saith the Lord . . . and [I] will be a Father unto you, and ye shall be my sons and daughters."
—2 CORINTHIANS 6:17–18

"Spiritual fatherhood fills the void and closes the gap of broken relationships between the old and the young."
—LARRY KREIDER,
THE CRY FOR SPIRITUAL FATHERS AND MOTHERS

"Peer pressure is simply living in the fear of man rather than in the fear of God."
—TEDD TRIPP, *SHEPHERDING A CHILD'S HEART*

"No wonder we lose our kids. We lose them because we fail to think clearly about man's chief end . . . to glorify God. In effect, we train them to think unbiblically."
—TEDD TRIPP, *SHEPHERDING A CHILD'S HEART*

"The great battle in life is not only to love God . . . but to keep Him on the throne of your heart, no matter what the world throws at you."

—TIM ROWE, *THE HEART*

"Virtues are the invisible elements of legacy so often taken for granted."

—DAVID GREEN

"The greater part of our legacies is made of invisible things."

—DAVID GREEN,
GIVING IT ALL AWAY . . . AND GETTING IT ALL BACK AGAIN

"The legacy we leave is not just in our possessions, but in the quality of our lives."

—BILLY GRAHAM

societal postscript

FATHERS

"An Endangered Species"

—WASHINGTON POST

FATHER ABSENCE may well be the most critical issue of our time. . . . We ignore the problem of father absence to our peril.

EDWARD KRUK, PHD, *PSYCHOLOGY TODAY*

THERE IS A CRISIS in America. According to the U.S. Census Bureau, 24 million children in America—one out of three—live without their biological dad in the home.

RYAN SANDERS, NATIONAL FATHERHOOD INITIATIVE

WHAT IS THE CAUSE?

DIVORCE. Since the sexual revolution of the 1960s and the launch of *no-fault* divorce in 1968, approximately one million children every year have been left as *virtual orphans*, placed almost exclusively in their mothers' homes.

UNWED PREGNANCY. Since the sexual revolution of the 1960s, cohabitation has exploded well over 1,000 percent. Cohabitation now exceeds marriage as the preferred and accepted form of male-female relationships, resulting in children born in serial relationships. Over 40 percent of America's children are now born out of wedlock.

> NOTE: That is in addition to the 57 million who have been aborted since 1973.

CULTURE FEMINIZATION. Since the sexual revolution of the 1960s, cultural leaders, in the name of sexual equality, have progressively demeaned men, masculinity and fathers as unnecessary in the lives of both women and children.

GOVERNMENT PARENTHOOD. Since the mid-1960s, in the growing divorce and sexually promiscuous culture, government has stepped in with well-intentioned programs to aid single mothers and to eradicate poverty, but has refused to deal with the underlying causes, resulting in devastating poverty and enforced separation of fathers from the home. This was a false compassion, destroying fatherhood, so that 70 percent of all black children are now born out of wedlock and arguably 85 percent do not live in a home with their biological father.

MALE ATTITUDES. Since the sexual revolution of the 1960s, men have increasingly seen women as objects of pleasure rather than partners in life, allowing government to replace us in the hearts and homes of our children. Many American fathers have, quite simply, stopped being real and responsible men. So, as one opinion writer opined, "The only question that remains is how much longer we are going to keep fooling ourselves?"

A CHURCH IN DEFAULT. At the root of all sociological and cultural analysis, perhaps the greatest and most lamentable cause of the carnage has been the wholesale abandonment by churches and pastors of historic biblical convictions, all since the sexual revolution of the 1960s. By far, the majority of pastors, congregations and denominations have changed teachings on divorce, remarriage and cohabitation, thus embracing the broader cultural patterns in a false pursuit of alleged compassion, thus making our churches complicit in the progressive undermining of both family and fatherhood.

WHAT ARE THE CONSEQUENCES?[1]

The curse causeless shall not come.

—PROVERBS 26:2

1. FATHER ABSENCE: Nearly 24 percent of U.S. children (17 million) now live in father-absent homes.

2. POVERTY: Children living in female-headed homes have a poverty rate of 48 percent, more than four times the rate for children living in homes with their fathers and mothers.

3. INFANT MORTALITY: Father absence has increased the rate of infant mortality of both black and white babies almost four times.

4. TEEN PREGNANCY: The pregnancy rate of adolescents between ages thirteen and eighteen is 164 percent higher in father-absent homes than in father-present homes.

5. GUN AND DRUG TRAFFICKING: Juvenile males in father-absent homes are 279 percent more likely to carry guns and engage in drug trafficking than those in father-present homes.

6. EDUCATION: Father absence is significantly related to lower educational attainment, particularly among black females.

7. CRIMINAL BEHAVIOR: According to the Bureau of Justice Statistics, the number of US children with an incarcerated father grew 79 percent from 1991 to 2007. Black fathers account for nearly half (46+ percent) of all children with an incarcerated father. This statistic instructively matches the fatherless facts, having only a remote relationship to racism.

CONCLUSION

There is a "father factor" in nearly all of the societal issues facing America today.

—NATIONAL FATHERHOOD INITIATIVE

taking my fatherly pulse

HOW WILL MY LIFE AFFECT THE NEXT TWO GENERATIONS?

HERE ARE SIMPLE TESTS TO determine my impact on the life of my nation, my community, my church, and my family:

1. As to my life DIRECTION:
    a. Who am I?
    b. Where have I been?
    c. What am I doing?
    d. Where am I going?
    e. Why am I doing what I do . . . or don't do?

2. As to my IMPACT:

    Am I part of the SOLUTION—or am I part of the PROBLEM?

3. As to my EXAMPLE:

a. How would my wife rate my spiritual leadership?

   (Poor) 1 2 3 4 5 6 7 8 9 10 (Excellent)

b. How would my children rate my spiritual leadership?

   (Poor) 1 2 3 4 5 6 7 8 9 10 (Excellent)

c. What is my degree of influence in the formation of my children's values? Compared to television?

   (Little) 1 2 3 4 5 6 7 8 9 10 (Great)

d. Do I underreport my income or overclaim my deductions on my tax return?

   (None of the time) 1 2 3 4 5 6 7 8 9 10 (Most of the time)

e. Do my wife, children, and others see me as a man of destiny and purpose?

   (None of the time) 1 2 3 4 5 6 7 8 9 10 (Most of the time)

f. Do those who know me believe that I am a man of integrity, of virtue, and of high moral character?

   (None of the time) 1 2 3 4 5 6 7 8 9 10 (Most of the time)

g. Do I spend quality time in prayer and in the study of God's Word daily?

   (None of the time) 1 2 3 4 5 6 7 8 9 10 (Most of the time)

How do I rate?

(Add each category in Item 3 and divide by 7.)

SAVE AMERICA MINISTRIES
Renewing moral and spiritual values that will
Restore national vision and purpose.
1 (800) SAVEUSA   *saveus.org*

about the author

FOR A VETERAN TRIAL ATTORNEY to be referred to as "a prophet for our time" is indeed unusual, but many who have heard Charles Crismier's daily radio broadcast, *Viewpoint*, believe just that. Now, in *Hearts of the Fathers*, his words, full of "passion and conviction," provide clear insight and direction in an increasingly chaotic, dangerous and deceptive world.

Crismier speaks from an unusual breadth of experience. After nine years as a public school teacher, he spent twenty years as a trial attorney, pleading causes before judge and jury. As a pastor's son, also serving in pastoral roles for thirty-five years, Crismier has been involved with ten distinct Protestant denominations—both mainline and otherwise, together with other independent and charismatic groups from coast to coast—providing an enviable insider's view of American Christianity and life as well as unique insight into world events.

Deeply troubled by the direction of America, Israel, the church and our world, this attorney left his Southern California law practice in 1992 to form Save America Ministries and was awarded the Valley Forge Freedom Foundation award for his contribution to the cause of "Rebuilding the Foundations of Faith and Freedom." Chuck probes the heart and conscience with both a rare combination of insight, directness, urgency and compassion, and a message that desperately needs to be heard and heeded before it is too late.

From the birthplace of America—Richmond, Virginia—this

attorney speaks provocatively and prophetically on daily national radio as "a Voice to the Church," declaring "Vision for the Nation" in America's greatest crisis hour, *preparing the way of the Lord* for history's final hour. That passion now pleads persuasively with the peoples, presidents, prime ministers, pundits and proclaimed religious leaders of our world in *Hearts of the Fathers*.

Charles Crismier can be contacted by writing or calling:

PO Box 70879
Richmond VA 23255
(804) 754-1822
crismier@saveus.org

or
visit his website:
www.saveus.org

notes

Chapter 1: Titanic Prophecy
1. David A. Kaplan and Anna Underwood, "The Iceberg Cometh," *Newsweek*, Nov. 25, 1996, pp.68-73.
2. Stephen Cox, *Richmond Times Dispatch*, April 15, 2001, p. F3.
3. David A. Kaplan and Anna Underwood, *Newsweek*, p. 69.
4. Ibid, p. 73.
5. Ibid, p. 69.
6. Bob Garner, "Lessons From the Titanic," *Focus on the Family*, April 1997, pp. 1-3.
7. Kim Masters, "Glub, Glub, Glub. . . ," *Time*, November 25, 1996, p. 104.
8. Bob Garner, "Lessons From the Titanic," *Focus on the Family*, p. 2.
9. Ibid, p. 3.
10. Graham Tibbetts, "Key That Could Have Saved the Titanic," *Telegraph*, August 30, 2007.
11. Brad Matsen, *Titanic's Last Secrets* (New York, Twelve, Hatchette Book Group, 2008), back cover.
12. Ibid.
13. Ibid, p. 227.
14. Ibid, p. 261.
15. Ibid, p. 238-39.
16. Ibid, p. 241.
17. Ibid, p. 239.
18. Ibid, p. 261.

Chapter 5: The Curse of Fatherlessness
1. Richard Ostling, "The Church Search," *Time*, April 5, 1993, http://content.time.com/time/magazine/article/0,9171,978164,00.html.

Chapter 7: Forsaking Our Fathers
1. Luke Rosiak, "Fathers Disappear from Households across America," *Washington Times*, December 25, 2012, http://www.washingtontimes.com/news/2012/dec/25/fathers-disappear-from-households-across-america/.
2. http://www.discoverthenetworks.org/viewSubCategory.asp?id=1261.
3. Ellen Goodman, "Abandonment of Children, of Parents—a Sad Portrait of Family," *Orlando Sentinel*, April 10, 1992, http://articles.orlandosentinel.com/1992-04-10/news/9204100331_1_father-american-children-abandon.

Chapter 9: The Fear of the Father
1. Ostling, "The Church Search" (see chap. 4, n. 1).
2. Steve Green, "God and God Alone," in *For God and God Alone*, Sparrow.

Chapter 12: The Folly of Fatherlessness
1. See Ray Williams, "The Decline of Fatherhood and the Male Identity Crisis," *Wired for Success* (blog), June 19, 2011, https://www.psychologytoday.com/blog/wired-success/201106/the-decline-fatherhood-and-the-male-identity-crisis; Alexander Mitscherlich, *Society Without a Father* (n.p.: Schocken, 1970); Guy Garcia, *The Decline of Men: How the American Male Is Getting Axed, Giving Up, and Flipping Off His Future* (New York: Harper Perennial, 2009), xii; David Blankenhorn, *Fatherless America: Confronting Our Most Urgent Social Problem* (New York: Harper Perennial, 1996), 1; *Newsweek*, August 30, 1993, issue.
2. Jessica Goodman, "Emmy winner Jill Soloway: Topple the Patriarchy," *Entertainment*, September 18, 2016, http://ew.com/article/2016/09/18/jill-soloway-topple-patriarchy-emmys/.
3. "The Extent of Fatherlessness," National Center for Fathering, accessed August 23, 2017, http://www.fathers.com/statistics-and-research/the-extent-of-fatherlessness/.
4. David Whitman, "The Trouble with Premarital Sex," *U.S. News & World Report*, May 19, 1997, 54–59.
5. Ibid.
6. Ibid.
7. Ibid.
8. Ibid.

Chapter 14: How to Leave a Godly Legacy
1. Goodman, "Emmy Winner Jill Soloway" (see chap. 11, n.).
2. For a more detailed and complete discussion of the fear of the Lord as woven through the entire Bible, see my titled *The SECRET of the Lord: The Hidden Truth That Defines Your Destiny* (n.p.: Elijah Books, 2011).

Chapter 16: False Fathers
1. John Cloud "7. Synthetic Authenticity," *Time*, March 13, 2008, http://content.time.com/time/specials/2007/article/0,28804,1720049_1720050_1722070,00.html.

Chapter 20: Fathering in Fearful Times
1. William Bentley Ball, *In Search of a National Morality: A Manifesto for Evangelicals and Catholics* (n.p.: Baker Book House, 1992), 12.
2. Alexandr Solzhenitsyn, speech delivered June 8, 1978, at Harvard University, available at the Online Speech Bank, at http://www.americanrhetoric.com/speeches/alexandersolzhenitsynharvard.htm.

Societal Postscript
1. http://fatherhoodfactor.com/us-fatherless-statistics/